THE
BIBLE
GUIDE

THE BIBLE GUIDE

A CONCISE OVERVIEW OF ALL 66 BOOKS

HOLMAN®

REFERENCE

NASHVILLE, TENNESSEE

The Bible Guide: A Concise Overview of All 66 Books
Edited and condensed by Ross H. McLaren

Copyright © 2018 by B&H Publishing Group
Nashville, Tennessee
All rights reserved.

ISBN: 978-1-4336-4889-2

Dewey Decimal Classification: 220.2
Subject Heading: BIBLE—
HANDBOOKS, MANUAL, ETC.

Printed in the United States of America

1 2 3 4 5 6 7 8 9 10 • 23 22 21 20 19 18

VP

CONTENTS

READING THE BIBLE FOR TRANSFORMATION

The apostle Paul encouraged the Roman believers, "Do not be conformed to this age, but be transformed by the renewing of your mind" (Rom 12:2). Here are five means by which we can appropriate the truth of Scripture for spiritual transformation.

READ THE BIBLE

Many Christians in the West do not know the books of the Bible, the Ten Commandments, or the events of Jesus's life. Much of this biblical illiteracy stems from a simple lack of *reading* Scripture. Make Bible reading a priority. Follow a Bible-reading plan. Very often, Bible reading ignites a greater love for reading. So take up and read!

MEMORIZE SCRIPTURE

Children stop memorizing Bible verses around middle-school age, never to pick it up again. Adults today, by and large, do not make the effort to memorize Scripture. The psalmist writes, "I have treasured your word in my heart so that I may not sin against you" (Ps 119:11). Oh how we need to write God's Word on the tablet of our hearts today! Here are a few suggestions: First, don't bite off more than you can chew. Before you set out to memorize the entire New Testament, start with a few verses. Second, ask others in your church or family to join you in keeping you accountable. Third, incorporate as many ways to memorize as possible—through music, writing verses out on paper, repetition, and other creative ideas.

MEDITATE ON SCRIPTURE

When we talk about "meditation," we are not talking about the Eastern religious practice of crossing your legs, saying "Om," and emptying your mind. Biblical meditation seeks to *fill* the mind with the truth, meaning, and application of the biblical text. In so doing, the Spirit of God aligns our minds with the mind of Christ so that we might be transformed into his likeness. Meditating on God's Word bears the fruit of a healthy and fruit-filled faith, which brings delight and godly perspective to your life and to the lives of those around you.

PRAY SCRIPTURE

Matthew Henry (1662–1714), the great Bible commentator, confined his prayers—almost entirely—to the language of

Scripture. Praying the Word of God to God not only provides God-honoring language but also transforms our souls in the process. By praying Scripture, we appropriate its truth in our thoughts and affections, which renews our minds and draws us heavenward. Filling our prayers with God's Word transforms our hearts by reflecting back to him the holiness and beauty of his revealed truth.

BECOME INVOLVED IN A COMMUNITY OF FAITH

In a local church believers are transformed through the faithful preaching of the Word, Bible study, small groups, counseling, and the many other contexts of Scripture-saturated edification. From accountability to encouragement, God has seen fit to equip you with the tools for gospel transformation within the community of faith.

As you read, memorize, meditate, and pray the Scriptures within the community of faith, may God plant you by streams of grace so that you may bear fruit in season, for his glory and your joy.

THE PENTATEUCH

The first five books of the Old Testament, sometimes called "the books of Moses," are also called the Pentateuch. Jewish tradition labeled these books collectively as the Torah, which means "teaching, instruction." In English Bibles these first five books are commonly called "Law." This designation is misleading. Large portions are not law at all; they are actually inspiring narratives.

The Pentateuch is one continuous narrative, but because of the physical limitations of scrolls, it was necessary to divide the narrative into five segments more easily manageable on leather or vellum scrolls. This division dates at least to the second century BC. The partitioning creates the unfortunate impression that these are distinct compositions to be interpreted separately. This is wrong. The story that begins in Genesis 1:1 climaxes with the making of the covenant at Sinai and ends with Moses's theological exposition of the covenant in Deuteronomy.

The pivotal event of the Pentateuch is God's revelation of himself at Sinai. Everything before is prologue, and all that comes after is epilogue. At Sinai the God of Abraham, Isaac, and Jacob formally became the God of Israel, binding Abraham's descendants to him by confirming the eternal covenant (Exod 31:16-17; Lev 24:8; cp. Judg 2:1).

The theological themes developed in the Pentateuch are God as Creator (Gen 1–2); God as Judge of sinful humanity, who spared Noah (Gen 3:1–10:32); God as the one who elected his agents of blessing the world, entered into covenant relationship with them, and promised to give the land of Canaan to their descendants as an eternal possession (Gen 11:37–50:26); God as the one who redeemed his people from slavery (Exod 1:1–15:21); God as the one who accompanied his people during their desert travels, providing for their physical needs and punishing the faithless (Exod 15:22–17:7; 18:1-27; Num 10:11–20:29); God as the one who entered into covenant relationship with and revealed his will comprehensively to Israel at Sinai (Exod 19:1–Num 10:10); God as the one who fights for Israel against their enemies (Exod 17:8-16; Num 22:1–25:18); God as the one who would give Israel their land and promised to be with them after the death of Moses (Num 26:1–Deut 34:12).

Jewish and Christian traditions almost unanimously recognize Moses as author of the Pentateuch; however, the fact remains that nowhere does the Pentateuch specifically name its author. As was common in the ancient Semitic world, it is anonymous. On the other hand, the internal evidence suggests that Moses kept a record of Israel's experiences in the desert (Exod 17:14; 24:4,7; 34:27; Num 33:1-2; Deut 31:9). Furthermore, many statements in the Old Testament credit the Pentateuch to Moses (e.g., Josh 1:7; 8:31-32; 1 Kgs 2:3;

2 Kgs 14:6; Ezra 6:18; Neh 13:1; Dan 9:11-13; Mal 4:4), and the New Testament identifies the Torah very closely with Moses (Matt 19:8; John 5:46-47; 7:19; Acts 3:22; Rom 10:5).

GENESIS

Author

Technically, Genesis is anonymous, but it is one of the five books (Genesis–Deuteronomy; the Pentateuch) associated with Moses by both Old Testament and New Testament writers.

Date

Moses, who lived in the 1400s BC, wrote Genesis, even though the events he recorded occurred long before his time and the book itself saw later editorial updates.

Big Picture

The God who created human beings and punished disobedience with death began his great plan of redemption with his covenant with Abraham and his descendants.

Summary

The book of Genesis is the book of beginnings in the Bible. Genesis ties together creation and human history, then largely narrowing its focus to the lives of Israel's famous patriarchs. Chapters 1–11 contain a selective history of the entire human race; chapters 12–50 tell the story of the direct ancestors of the Israelites. Within those two broad divisions, chapters 1–2 deal with creation, while chapter 3 tells of the entrance of sin into the world. Chapters 6–9 detail the great flood and the preservation of Noah and his family, after which God scattered people over the face of the earth (chaps. 10–11). God's plan for redemption centered in Abraham (12:1-3) and continued through Isaac, Jacob, and Joseph, whose lives and works are narrated in chapters 12–50.

Key Verses

"In the beginning God created the heavens and the earth" (Gen 1:1).

"Abram believed the LORD, and he credited it to him as righteousness" (Gen 15:6).

Food for Thought

God is the sovereign Lord and Creator of all things whose control over human history is so complete that even the worst of human deeds can be turned to serve his benevolent purposes (50:20).

Takeaway

Through Genesis we understand where we came from, how we got in the fallen state we are in, and the beginnings of God's plan of salvation on our behalf.

EXODUS

Author

Technically, Exodus is anonymous, but it is one of the five books (Genesis—Deuteronomy; the Pentateuch) associated with Moses by both Old Testament and New Testament writers.

Date

Moses wrote Exodus sometime between 1445 BC and 1406 BC.

Big Picture

When God redeemed his chosen people Israel through his servant Moses, he entered into a covenant relationship with them and instituted a place of dwelling with them—the tabernacle.

Summary

Exodus records God's act of saving the Israelites and establishing them as a covenant community, a nation chosen to serve and represent him. Exodus describes the enslavement and oppression of the Israelites (chap. 1); the preparation and call of Moses (chaps. 2–4); the conflict between Yahweh, the God of Israel, and the gods of Egypt (represented by Pharaoh) in the 10 plagues and institution of the Passover (chaps. 5–13); the exodus of the Israelites from Egypt (chaps. 14–18); their establishment as a nation in covenant with the Lord and the giving of the Ten Commandments and other laws (chaps. 19–23); Israel's rebellion (chaps. 32–34); and the Lord's provision for their ongoing relationship, symbolized by his presence at the tabernacle the Israelites built for him (chaps. 24–31; 35–40).

Key Verses

"That day the LORD saved Israel from the power of the Egyptians, and Israel saw the Egyptians dead on the seashore. When Israel saw the great power that the LORD used against the Egyptians, the people feared the LORD and believed in him and in his servant Moses" (Exod 14:30-31).

"I am the LORD your God, who brought you out of the land of Egypt, out of the place of slavery. Do not have other gods besides me" (Exod 20:2-3).

Food for Thought

The book of Exodus shows God at work with the goal of having close fellowship with people whom he made his treasured possession and through whom he would bless the world. He rescued the Israelites in order to make himself known, not only by the exercise of his power but also through an ongoing covenant relationship based on his capacity for patience, grace, and forgiveness. The record of what the Lord did for the Israelites provided grounds for them to recognize him as their God who deserved their complete loyalty and obedience.

Takeaway

Just as God delivered the Israelites who were under the protection of the blood of the Passover lamb from physical slavery in Egypt, so Jesus delivers those who trust in the death of the true Passover Lamb from slavery to sin.

LEVITICUS

Author

Technically, Leviticus is anonymous, but it is one of the five books (Genesis—Deuteronomy; the Pentateuch) associated with Moses by both Old Testament and New Testament writers.

Date

Moses wrote Leviticus sometime between 1445 BC and 1406 BC.

Big Picture

When God forgives people their sins and declares them holy, he then expects them to live in fellowship with him by following his regulations concerning separated holy living.

Summary

Leviticus sets forth God's means of grace by which a sinful people can stay in right relationship with him. Forgiveness is granted through right sacrifices offered the right way by the right priests. God's people maintain fellowship with him by living according to his regulations and being separate from the moral corruption of the world around them. Chapters 1–7 deal with the nature, purpose, and rituals of sacrifice. Chapters 8–10 describe the establishment of the priesthood. The laws concerning what was clean and unclean (chaps. 11–15) were designed to remind Israel that it was to be separate from the world. The annual Day of Atonement (chap. 16) reminded Israel of its need for purification by having its sins covered and removed. The "Holiness Code" in chapters 17–25 focuses on the moral holiness of the people. A warning about blessings and curses and instructions about consecration, or dedication, offerings close the book (chaps. 26–27).

Key Verses

"For I am the LORD, who brought you up from the land of Egypt to be your God, so you must be holy because I am holy" (Lev 11:45).

"The LORD spoke to Moses: 'Speak to the entire Israelite community and tell them: Be holy because I, the LORD your God, am holy'" (Lev 19:1-2).

"You are to be holy to me because I, the LORD, am holy, and I have set you apart from the nations to be mine" (Lev 20:26).

Food for Thought

Leviticus is primarily a collection of laws. These laws can be divided into two groups. First are the commands. These are both positive ("You must . . .") and negative ("You must not . . ."). The second type of laws is case law using an example of what to do if such-and-such happened ("If a man . . ."). God also gave further civil laws, moral laws, and ceremonial laws to help his people know how to live holy lives in community.

Takeaway

God's people are to reflect his holiness in every aspect of their lives and in all their relationships.

NUMBERS

Author

Technically, Numbers is anonymous, but it is one of the five
books (Genesis—Deuteronomy; the Pentateuch) associated
with Moses by both Old Testament and New Testament
writers.

Date

Moses wrote Numbers sometime between 1445 BC and 1406
BC.

Big Picture

God used Moses to lead Israel from Sinai to Kadesh. After
Israel rejected him there by not entering the promised land,
resulting in 40 years of wilderness wandering, God remained
faithful and led a new generation to the edge of the promised
land.

Summary

Numbers answers the questions: How did Israel get from
Mount Sinai to the border of the promised land? and Why
did the journey take so long? The book contrasts God's
faithfulness with Israel's disobedience. Numbers opens with
a census that reveals God had blessed Israel with the strength
necessary to conquer the promised land (chaps. 1–2). This is
followed by organization of the nation for worship (chaps.
3–4), instructions for preserving the purity of God's people
(chaps. 5–6), and the building of the tabernacle (chaps.
7–9). As Israel traveled, they grumbled against Moses and
his leadership (chaps. 10–12). Spies were sent into the land,

but Israel rejected God's plan to bring the nation into the promised land (chaps. 13–14). Thus Israel was condemned to wander in the wilderness for 40 years until that generation died off and God again brought the next generation to the edge of the promised land (chaps. 15–36).

Key Verses

"Whenever the cloud was lifted up above the tent, the Israelites would set out; at the place where the cloud stopped, there the Israelites camped" (Num 9:17).

"I, the Lord, have spoken. I swear that I will do this to the entire evil community that has conspired against me. They will come to an end in the wilderness, and there they will die" (Num 14:35).

Food for Thought

A key turning point in Numbers is when the Lord commanded Moses to send a leader from each of the 12 tribes to scout out the land of Canaan. Ten of these leaders came back and said it would be impossible for Israel to take possession of the land. Joshua and Caleb brought a minority report that Israel certainly could possess the land (chaps. 13–14). The majority ruled, with the result that Israel wandered in the wilderness for 40 years.

Takeaway

The experience of the Israelites in the book of Numbers shows there are consequences to disobedience, but God's grace remains, and his redemptive plan and desire for his people will not be stopped.

DEUTERONOMY

Author

Moses (1:1,5; 31:24-26).

Date

Moses wrote Deuteronomy sometime before 1406 BC; however the book saw later editorial updates.

Big Picture

Through Moses's great speeches near the end of his life, God reminded Israel on the verge of entering the promised land about his mighty acts, his covenant, and his many commandments.

Summary

Deuteronomy consists of Moses's four farewell messages to a new generation of Israelites. The setting is 40 years after the exodus from Egypt. Israel is poised to enter the promised land. In these farewell messages Moses pleads passionately with his people to keep God at the center of their national life once they begin to take possession of the land. In Moses's first address (1:6–4:40) he recounted Israel's journeys in the wilderness and stressed the need for obedience. In his second address (4:44–28:68) Moses taught lessons from the law, giving instructions for life in the land of Canaan. His third address (29:1–30:20) focused on covenant renewal and blessings and curses. Moses's final address (31:1–29) was his farewell message. The Song of Moses is recorded in 31:30–32:52, his blessing on Israel in chapter 33, and his death in chapter 34.

Key Verses

"Listen, Israel: The Lord our God, the Lord is one. Love the Lord your God with all your heart, with all your soul, and with all your strength" (Deut 6:4-5).

"For I am commanding you today to love the Lord your God, to walk in his ways, and to keep his commands, statutes, and ordinances, so that you may live and multiply, and the Lord your God may bless you in the land you are entering to possess" (Deut 30:16).

"I call heaven and earth as witnesses against you today that I have set before you life and death, blessing and curse. Choose life so that you and your descendants may live, love the Lord your God, obey him, and remain faithful to him. For he is your life, and he will prolong your days as you live in the land the Lord swore to give to your fathers Abraham, Isaac, and Jacob" (Deut 30:19-20).

Food for Thought

A chief task of the people of God is conveying to the next generation who God is, what he has done, and his requirements. Moses charges Israel with taking to heart their confession of faith, the Shema (6:4-5). He further enjoins them to keep God's Word before them, letting it shape everyday conversations and actions within the family (6:7-9).

Takeaway

God's words are not empty expressions but are a matter of life and death.

THE HISTORICAL BOOKS

The Historical Books in the English Bible are Joshua, Judges, Ruth, 1 and 2 Samuel, 1 and 2 Kings, 1 and 2 Chronicles, Ezra, Nehemiah, and Esther. This continuous narrative traces the history of Israel from the conquest of Canaan by Joshua (about 1400 BC) to the restoration of the Jews during the Persian period (about 400 BC)—about a thousand years of Israel's history. These books cover the years of Israel's conquest and settlement of the promised land under Joshua, the leadership of the judges over the tribes of Israel, the reigns of the kings during both the united kingdom and the divided kingdoms, the fall of the northern kingdom at the hands of the Assyrians, the captivity of the southern kingdom in Babylon, and the Jews' return to Jerusalem after 70 years of exile.

At first, the books of 1 and 2 Samuel were one book, as were 1 and 2 Kings, 1 and 2 Chronicles, and Ezra-Nehemiah. The Septuagint—the oldest Greek translation of the Old Testament—was the first to divide the books. Our English Bibles follow the Septuagint and arrange the Historical

Books in a loosely chronological order. The Hebrew canon arranges the Historical Books differently. The Hebrew canon consists of three divisions (Law, Prophets, and Writings). Joshua, Judges, 1 and 2 Samuel, and 1 and 2 Kings are in the Prophets. Within this division they are designated the Former Prophets (the Latter Prophets are Isaiah, Jeremiah, Ezekiel, and the twelve Minor Prophets). First and Second Chronicles, Ezra, and Nehemiah occur in the Writings as the final four books of the Hebrew canon, with Chronicles coming last. The books of Ruth and Esther also appear in the Writings in the Hebrew Bible.

The heading the "Former Prophets" for Joshua, Judges, Samuel, and Kings indicates that the Jews did not read these books as histories in our modern sense. Although written in narrative form, they were *prophetic*. Like the oracles of the Latter Prophets, these "histories" declare the word of the Lord. They interpret Israel's history from the theological perspective of God's covenant with Israel. As prophetic writings, they present God's evaluation and verdict on the history of Israel.

First and Second Chronicles and Ezra-Nehemiah give a different but complementary perspective from Joshua through 2 Kings on Israel's history. First and Second Chronicles parallel this first history from creation to the destruction of Jerusalem. Ezra-Nehemiah continues the account with the return of the exiles from Babylon and the restoration of the religious life of Judah (about 400 BC). Since these books were written during and after the exile, they focus on the religious life of restored Israel. Temple worship and observance of the law of Moses are particularly emphasized.

Ruth and Esther, classified as historical books in English Bibles, are included by the Jews among the Writings. Ruth, set at the harvest, is read at the Festival of Weeks (Pentecost), which celebrates the spring ingathering (May–June). Esther's story gives the origins of the Festival of Purim and is read on that occasion (Adar 14–15 [Feb.–Mar.]).

JOSHUA

Author

The book of Joshua is named for the most famous member
of the Israelites in the generation after the death of Moses;
however, the author of the book of Joshua is not identified
in the Bible. Jewish tradition assigned the book to Joshua.
Samuel is another possibility.

Date

If written shortly after the events it records, the book can be
dated to about 1375 BC; if written by Samuel, then 1050 BC.

Big Picture

The book describes the history of the generation of Israel
who crossed the Jordan River and entered the promised land
of Canaan, defeated their adversaries, saw the division of the
land into the tribal allotments, and renewed the covenant
between God and themselves.

Summary

The book of Joshua documents the conquest and settlement
of the land of Canaan. The book naturally divides into four
main sections: crossing over the Jordan River (chaps. 1–5);
taking the land (chaps. 6–12); dividing the land (chaps.
13–21); worshipping the Lord (chaps. 22–24). The first five
chapters focus on the preparations Joshua and the Israelites
made to cross over the Jordan River and invade the land.
Chapters 6–12 record the three-part campaign—central,
southern, northern—of Joshua and the Israelites to claim the
promised land as their inheritance. The most famous victory

was their first—at Jericho. Chapters 13–21 document the inheritance and distribution of the promised land to Israel's tribes. The final section of the book focuses on the farewell speeches of Joshua and the consecration of the land through the great covenant renewal ceremony at Shechem.

Key Verses

"This book of instruction must not depart from your mouth; you are to meditate on it day and night so that you may carefully observe everything written in it. For then you will prosper and succeed in whatever you do" (Josh 1:8).

"But if it doesn't please you to worship the LORD, choose for yourselves today: Which will you worship—the gods your fathers worshiped beyond the Euphrates River or the gods of the Amorites in whose land you are living? As for me and my family, we will worship the LORD" (Josh 24:15).

Food for Thought

The name *Joshua* means "The Lord is salvation." It is the Hebrew equivalent of the name *Jesus*. As Jesus saves us by faith in his shed blood and makes us members of his family, so under Joshua, Rahab the harlot was saved by grace through faith as evidenced by her display of a scarlet cord. Just as Joshua led the people to victory over their enemies, so Jesus leads us to daily victory over our adversaries—the world, the flesh, and the devil. As the Old Testament Joshua led God's people over the Jordan into their promised land, so our greater Joshua, Jesus, leads us into our promised land—eternal glory (Heb 2:10).

Takeaway

To follow God faithfully throughout our time on earth, we must courageously obey the entire Word of God and keep our eyes focused on the commander of the Lord's army, the Lord Jesus Christ.

JUDGES

Author

No author is named in the book of Judges, but Jewish traditional assigned it to Samuel.

Date

The events described in Judges are to be dated from 1350 BC to 1050 BC. If recorded by Samuel, it would have been written around 1050 BC.

Big Picture

Throughout the period between the conquest and the rise of the monarchy, Israel experienced a repeated cycle of apostasy, oppression, repentance, and restoration through the work of divinely appointed judges.

Summary

The book of Judges falls into three parts: a prologue that deals with the failure of the second generation to press on with the conquest of Canaan (1:1–3:6), a sixfold cycle of sin and salvation through a deliverer or judge God raised up (3:7–16:31), and an appendix that shows the full effects of total depravity let loose upon the people (chaps. 17–21). After Israel's conquest of the land, Israel entered a time of apostasy. The book of Judges describes recurrences of a cycle with predictable phases. First, the people sinned against the Lord and fell into idolatry. Second, the Lord raised up an adversary to afflict them and turn them back to him. Third, the people cried out to the Lord in repentance. Fourth, the Lord brought deliverance for them through a judge whom he raised up, even though each was seriously flawed. The stories of Deborah, Gideon, Jephthah, and Samson are most memorable.

Key Verses

"Whenever the LORD raised up a judge for the Israelites, the LORD was with him and saved the people from the power of their enemies while the judge was still alive" (Judg 2:18).

"In those days there was no king in Israel; everyone did whatever seemed right to him" (Judg 17:6 and 21:25).

Food for Thought

The seven cycles of Israel's vacillation between obedience and rebellion point to the fundamental problem in the book of Judges—Israel's loss of the memory of the Lord's redemptive work on their behalf. Judges thus illustrates the fundamental problem of the human heart—when God's people forget his saving acts, they go after other gods. Judges makes clear the link between spiritual commitment and ethical conduct.

Takeaway

When people are allowed to do whatever they want without any restrictions, the result will be moral and spiritual chaos for both individuals and society.

RUTH

Author

Jewish tradition attributes the authorship of Ruth to Samuel, but the book itself, named for the heroine of the story, offers no hint of the identity of its author.

Date

The book of Ruth is set "during the time of the judges" (1:1), the time between the conquest of the land under Joshua and the rise of King David, whose family records form the conclusion of the book. It is not clear exactly when during the time of the judges the book belongs. Perhaps it was written about 950 BC.

Big Picture

Ruth, a Moabite widow, found love and fulfillment through Boaz, a rich Israelite bachelor who redeemed the ancestral land and the name of Ruth's deceased husband, thereby restoring Naomi, Ruth's mother-in-law, from emptiness to fullness.

Summary

The book of Ruth is a beautiful story of devastating loss, loyal commitment, and wonderful redemption. Naomi thought the Lord's hand of judgment was upon her after she and her husband left the promised land in search of food and married their sons to Moabite women. She underestimated God's grace. Her daughter-in-law Ruth turned out to be the means by which the Lord would meet her needs for food and offspring to carry on the family name. Upon returning to

Bethlehem, Ruth's choice of a place to glean, which seemed to be a matter of chance, turned out to be a divine appointment with Boaz, an important and wealthy relative to Naomi's deceased husband. Boas fulfilled the role of family redeemer for Naomi and Ruth.

Key Verses

"Ruth replied: Don't plead with me to abandon you or to return and not follow you. For wherever you go, I will go, and wherever you live, I will live; your people will be my people, and your God will be my God. Where you die, I will die, and there I will be buried. May the LORD punish me, and do so severely, if anything but death separates you and me" (Ruth 1:16-17).

"The women said to Naomi, 'Blessed be the LORD, who has not left you without a family redeemer today. May his name become well known in Israel'" (Ruth 4:14).

Food for Thought

A correlation may be made between the redemption of Ruth by Boaz and the redemption of sinners by Christ. Because of God's covenant faithfulness, he has provided the Redeemer we all need in Jesus Christ. Jesus is the true King toward whom the family records of David will ultimately extend (Matt 1:5-6), and he is the Redeemer from Bethlehem in whom his wandering people find rest. In him the Gentiles too are incorporated into the people of God by faith and are granted a place in the family of promise.

Takeaway

Even though we have wandered away from the Lord and ended up empty and alone, the Lord's design is to redeem us—to bring us back to him and replace our emptiness with a new fullness.

1 SAMUEL

Author

The book names no author, but some scholars believe Samuel was largely responsible for the material up to 1 Samuel 25 and that the prophets Nathan and Gad gave significant input to the rest (based on 1 Chr 29:29). First and Second Samuel originally were one book.

Date

First Samuel may have been written during Solomon's reign, about 950 BC, but 1 Samuel 27:6 may suggest the book was not completed until perhaps a few generations after the division of the kingdom in 930 BC.

Big Picture

After Samuel's leadership as a judge, the people of Israel turned to Saul as their first king, whom God later rejected and instead chose David, who had many adventures as a renegade from Saul's court.

Summary

First Samuel is organized around three great men and tells their stories successively. The first seven chapters describe Samuel's birth, call, and ministry as a prophet and as the last judge among the Israelites. Chapter 8 is a major turning point as the people ask for a king to rule them "the same as all the other nations have" (8:5). Chapters 9–12 then describe Saul's selection as Israel's first king—at God's direction, yet not his perfect will for the time (12:16-18). Chapters 13–31 describe Saul's victories and failures. Saul was a king with great physical stature and military skill (14:47-52), but his heart was not one with the Lord (13:14). His unwillingness to obey the Lord's commands ultimately outweighed his accomplishments, and chapters 16–31 describe his reign's downward spiral.

Key Verses

"Therefore, this is the declaration of the LORD, the God of Israel: 'I did say that your family and your forefather's family would walk before me forever. But now,' this is the LORD's declaration, 'no longer! For those who honor me I will honor, but those who despise me will be disgraced'" (1 Sam 2:30).

"Then Samuel said: Does the LORD take pleasure in burnt offerings and sacrifices as much as in obeying the LORD? Look: to obey is better than sacrifice, to pay attention is better than the fat of rams" (1 Sam 15:22).

Food for Thought

Saul's rule highlights the dangers to which the Israelites fell victim as they clamored for a king to lead them. Samuel's warnings fell on deaf ears (8:10-20) because God's people were intent on becoming like the nations around them. In the end they got exactly what they asked for, but they paid a terrible price. Saul's life stands as a warning that we should trust God's timing for life's provisions and not demand that God do what we want just so we can be like others.

Takeaway

When leaders focus their attention on the Lord and see their leadership roles as instruments for his glory, they flourish; when they abandon the Lord and use their offices for their own gain, they fail—and lead their people down with them.

2 SAMUEL

Author

The book names no author, but some scholars (based on 1 Chr 29:29) believe the prophets Nathan and Gad gave significant input to the composition.

Date

Second Samuel was written sometime after the reign of King David (1010–970 BC), perhaps during Solomon's reign, about 950 BC. First and Second Samuel originally were one book.

Big Picture

David's reign over Israel included times of elation, such as his conquest of Jerusalem and the Lord's promise of an everlasting dynasty, as well as times of failure, such as his adultery with Bathsheba and the treason of his son Absalom.

Summary

Second Samuel has three clear sections: David's triumphs (chaps. 1–10), David's transgressions (chap. 11), and David's troubles (chaps. 12–24). Chapters 1–4 describe the struggle for Israel's throne that began with Saul's death. Chapters 5–24 present highlights of David's reign. In the theological centerpiece of the book, God instituted a special covenant with David, promising an eternal lineage who would rule on an eternal throne over an everlasting kingdom (7:1-29). David's sin with Bathsheba (chaps. 11–12), however, brought disastrous consequences to his reign, including the rebellion of his own son Absalom (chaps. 15–18) and that of a Benjaminite named Sheba (chap. 20). In the end David's repentance confirmed his designation as a man after God's heart, but his sin showed that breaking God's laws can lead to many unforeseen long-term, catastrophic consequences. The last section of the book is an appendix about David's career (chaps. 21–24).

Key Verses

"Your house and kingdom will endure before me forever, and your throne will be established forever" (2 Sam 7:16).

"David responded to Nathan, 'I have sinned against the LORD.' Then Nathan replied to David, 'And the LORD has taken away your sin; you will not die'" (2 Sam 12:13).

"The LORD is my rock, my fortress, and my deliverer" (2 Sam 22:2).

Food for Thought

David's rule testified to the amazing works the Lord could and would do through a life yielded to him. Israel's second king seemed well aware of God's blessing on his life and displayed a tender heart toward the things of God (5:12; 7:1-2; 22:1-51; 23:1-7). However, the consequences of David's sin with Bathsheba stand as a warning to all who experience sin's attraction. God holds his children accountable for their actions, and even forgiven sin can have terrible consequences.

Takeaway

David's reflection in Psalm 51 on his adulterous affair and confrontation with Nathan the prophet—including his shame, repentance, confession, and restoration—is unsurpassed in Scripture on the relationship between heartbroken confession of sin and divine forgiveness and stands as a profound paradigm of salvation even for today.

1 KINGS

Author

No author is named, but Jewish tradition suggested Jeremiah as a possible author. Whoever the author was, he states that he drew on earlier primary sources, specifically mentioning "the Book of Solomon's Events" (11:41), "the Historical Record of Israel's Kings" (14:19), and "the Historical Record of Judah's Kings" (14:29).

Date

First Kings covers the years 970 BC to 852 BC. First and Second Kings originally were one book that was divided into two books in the second century BC.

Big Picture

First Kings tells the story of the end of David's kingdom; the rise, expansion, and splendor of Solomon's great empire; the division of Israel into the two kingdoms of Judah and Israel (Ephraim) after Solomon's death; the beginning of the two nations' representative histories; and the prophetic and miraculous ministry of the prophet Elijah.

Summary

First Kings divides into two clear sections: chapters 1–11 cover the united kingdom, and chapters 12–22 begin the story of the divided kingdom. As King Solomon began his reign, he realized that in order to govern he needed more than human wisdom. He humbly asked God for such wisdom (chap. 3). Solomon was able to undertake numerous building projects, in particular the Jerusalem temple. He became an important international figure through wealth, trade, and politics. The foreign wives Solomon married turned his heart away from total devotion to the Lord (chaps. 4–11). Under Solomon's son Rehoboam the kingdom was torn in two in 930 BC. The once-united nation of Israel then entered a downward spiral (chaps. 12–16). The ten northern tribes became the nation of Israel (Ephraim), and the two southern tribes (Judah and Benjamin) became the nation of Judah. Chapters 17–22 tell of the miracle-working prophet Elijah and his ministry.

Key Verses

"God gave Solomon wisdom, very great insight, and understanding as vast as the sand on the seashore" (1 Kgs 4:29).

"When all Israel saw that the king [Rehoboam] had not listened to them, the people answered him: What portion do we have in David? We have no inheritance in the son of Jesse. Israel, return to your tents; David, now look after your own house!" (1 Kgs 12:16).

Food for Thought

Solomon began his reign by seeking wisdom from the Lord and exercising that wisdom in impressive ways (chap. 3). Nevertheless, along the way Solomon allowed himself to be distracted from the Lord's wisdom and ways and fell into disobedience, which resulted in division and generations of future kings following his negative example. The history of the two kingdoms shows us that as lived their leaders, so lived the people. On the other hand, the ministry of the prophet Elijah teaches us what God can do through one person who takes a stand for him.

Takeaway

No matter how humbly or devotedly a person starts out
following the Lord, or what great deeds that person does for
the Lord, it is not as important as how he or she finishes the
course.

2 KINGS

Author

No author is named. Jewish tradition suggests Jeremiah as a possible author. Whoever the author was, he states that he drew on earlier primary sources, specifically mentioning "the Historical Record of Israel's Kings" (1:18) and "the Historical Record of Judah's Kings" (8:23).

Date

The final stage of composition or compilation had to come after the release of Jehoiachin from Babylonian imprisonment (ca. 562 BC; see 25:27-30), and before Cyrus's edict of 539 BC. Second Kings covers the years 852 BC to 562 BC. First and Second Kings originally were one book that was divided into two books in the second century BC.

Big Picture

Even after Elisha's ministry, Israel persisted in idolatry and so went into permanent captivity; yet Judah, despite the prophets and few righteous kings, continued to be so wicked that God sent Nebuchadnezzar to remove them to Babylon.

Summary

Second Kings continues the story from 1 Kings, picking up with the death of Israel's king Ahaziah in 852 BC, summarizing the histories of the rest of Israel's and Judah's kings, relating the fall of Israel to Assyria in 722 BC, and finishing with the fall of the southern kingdom to Babylon in 586 BC and its aftermath. In the midst of these events occurred the prophetic ministry of the prophet Elisha (chaps.

1–8). King Jehu's dynasty rid northern Israel of its Baalism, but the slide to destruction came quickly afterwards with the rise and fall of four dynasties within the short span of 30 years (chaps. 1–17). Meanwhile, in Judah, after the fall of Israel, the reigns of Hezekiah (18:1–20:21) and Josiah (22:1–23:30) brought sweeping moral and religious reforms that prolonged Judah's existence for more than a hundred years. However, under Judah's most wicked king, Manasseh (21:1-26), and his evil successors (23:31–25:7) Judah fell under God's final judgment and was conquered by the Babylonians (25:8-30).

Key Verses

"The Israelites persisted in all the sins that Jeroboam committed and did not turn away from them. Finally, the LORD removed Israel from his presence just as he had declared through all his servants the prophets. So Israel has been exiled to Assyria from their homeland to this very day" (2 Kgs 17:22-23).

"On the seventh day of the fifth month—which was the nineteenth year of King Nebuchadnezzar of Babylon—Nebuzaradan, the captain of the guards, a servant of the king of Babylon, entered Jerusalem. He burned the LORD's temple, the king's palace, and all the houses of Jerusalem; he burned down all the great houses. The whole Chaldean army with the captain of the guards tore down the walls surrounding Jerusalem" (2 Kgs 25:8-10).

Food for Thought

While many people may think they are OK with God by their own standards, the books of Kings teach us that God evaluates people by just one criterion—did they do right in the eyes of the Lord? Tragically, for the most part, many people do not. And so God's verdict against the last king of Judah should be a warning to all: "Zedekiah did what was evil in the LORD's sight just as Jehoiakim had done. Because of the LORD's anger, it came to the point in Jerusalem and Judah that he finally banished them from his presence" (24:19-20).

Takeaway

God's punishment on people for their sins often does not occur immediately; this does not mean it will not come eventually. God's delay is for our salvation; he gives people time to repent and reform their ways. If they do not, his punishment is sure to come.

1 CHRONICLES

Author

No author is named. Jewish tradition suggests Ezra was the author. The author states that he drew on earlier primary sources, specifically mentioning "the Book of the Kings of Israel" (9:1) and "the Events of the Seer Samuel, the Events of the Prophet Nathan, and the Events of the Seer Gad" (29:29).

Date

Around 450 BC, after the return of the Jewish exiles from Babylon. Like 1 and 2 Samuel and 1 and 2 Kings, 1 and 2 Chronicles originally was one book that was divided into two books in the second century BC.

Big Picture

David ruled for 40 years under the blessing of God, lavishing his attention on Jerusalem, the priesthood, and preparation for building the temple.

Summary

A lengthy section of genealogical material, the most extensive found in Scripture, begins the book of 1 Chronicles (chaps. 1–9). An important function of the genealogies, which trace the history of Israel from its ancestral roots in Adam to the period of restoration after the Babylonian exile, was to show continuity in God's plan for Israel. King David's rule was glorious, and the pinnacle of his reign was his bringing of the ark of the covenant into Jerusalem (chap. 15). God honored David's desire to build a temple by granting him an eternal throne (chap. 17). While David was not allowed to build

God's temple, he did make preparations for its construction (chaps. 22–29). For the Chronicler, this was David's most important contribution and governed his account of David's reign.

Key Verses

"I will appoint him over my house and my kingdom forever, and his throne will be established forever" (1 Chr 17:14).

"Yet the LORD God of Israel chose me out of all my father's family to be king over Israel forever. For he chose Judah as leader, and from the house of Judah, my father's family, and from my father's sons, he was pleased to make me king over all Israel" (1 Chr 28:4).

Food for Thought

Times were difficult and disappointing for those who returned from the Babylonian exile. Many wondered whether they still fit into God's plan or whether God's promises were still applicable to them. The author of 1 Chronicles addressed such concerns by showing that even though a Davidic king was not on a temporal throne, they still were God's people and could still wait in hope for total restoration. And while waiting, they could still do the things God required, such as offering the right sacrifices with the right priests at the right place. Such lessons would keep them from making the same mistakes as those who came before them.

Takeaway

As we live our lives, we should have as a primary goal to build God's eternal kingdom, not our own.

2 CHRONICLES

Author

No author is named. Jewish tradition suggests Ezra was the author. The author states that he drew on earlier primary sources, specifically mentioning "the Book of the Kings of Judah and Israel" (16:11), "the Events of Jehu son of Hanani" (20:34), and "the Visions of the Prophet Isaiah son of Amoz" (32:32).

Date

Around 450 BC, after the return of the Jewish exiles from Babylon. Like 1 and 2 Samuel and 1 and 2 Kings, 1 and 2 Chronicles originally was one book that was divided into two books in the second century BC.

Big Picture

After Solomon's glorious reign, which culminated in the dedication of the temple, kings of the Davidic dynasty—some righteous and some evil—continued ruling in Jerusalem until the destruction of the temple and the exile of the people to Babylon.

Summary

Second Chronicles covers four and a half centuries, from the start of Solomon's reign (ca. 971 BC) to Cyrus's edict that freed the Jews from captivity (539 BC). The building of the temple is the central concern of 2 Chronicles (chaps. 2–7). The book begins with Solomon's plans to build the temple in Jerusalem and ends with its destruction. In between these events an account of the kings of Judah is given from the perspective of how temple worship fared under them (chaps. 10–36). Special attention is called to those kings (Asa, Joash, Hezekiah, and Josiah) who initiated repairs to the temple and led the nation in religious reform and renewal. The book ends with Cyrus the Persian's ordering the rebuilding of the temple.

Key Verses

"When Solomon finished praying, fire descended from heaven and consumed the burnt offering and the sacrifices, and the glory of the Lord filled the temple" (2 Chr 7:1).

"This is what King Cyrus of Persia says: The Lord, the God of the heavens, has given me all the kingdoms of the earth and has appointed me to build him a temple at Jerusalem in Judah. Any of his people among you may go up, and may the Lord his God be with him" (2 Chr 36:23).

Food for Thought

The thrust of 2 Chronicles is the building, dedication, and honoring of the Lord's temple by both kings and people. The New Testament teaches believers that our bodies are God's temple and we will be judged by how we honor him with them (1 Cor 3:16-17; 6:19-20; 2 Cor 6:16).

Takeaway

Second Chronicles focuses at length on Solomon, whose splendid rule in Jerusalem is a preview of Christ's everlasting reign in the new Jerusalem (Matt 12:42; Rev 21–22).

EZRA

Author

The book is named for Ezra, the leading character, to whom Jewish tradition ascribed the authorship.

Date

Around 430 BC, after two successive waves of Jewish exiles returned from Babylon. Ezra and Nehemiah originally were one book that was divided into two books in the fourth century AD.

Big Picture

The book of Ezra relates the story of two groups of Jews who returned from the Babylonian captivity to live in Jerusalem and what happened to them.

Summary

The first section of Ezra (chaps. 1–6) provides an account of the first group of 40,000 Jews who in 538 BC returned to Jerusalem from captivity in Babylon—just then under the rule of Cyrus the Persian. Their main objective was to rebuild the temple. They laid the temple's foundation in 536 BC, but opposition from enemies stopped the work. After a long delay the returnees finished the temple in 515 BC and celebrated its dedication with joy (6:16). Sixty years are passed over in silence until Ezra and a small group of less than 2,000 Jews returned to Jerusalem in 458 BC. Their story is told in chapters 7–10. Ezra had been granted unusual power and authority over Jerusalem by King Artaxerxes of Persia. Ezra was distressed when he discovered the spiritual condition of the people and led them into a renewed covenant relationship with God through teaching them the law of God.

Key Verses

"Then the Israelites, including the priests, the Levites, and the rest of the exiles, celebrated the dedication of the house of God with joy" (Ezra 6:16).

"Now Ezra had determined in his heart to study the law of the LORD, obey it, and teach its statutes and ordinances in Israel" (Ezra 7:10).

Food for Thought

God is righteous and acts on behalf of his people. This may include working through pagan kings, who issue decrees and make laws, as well as through godly teachers, who faithfully teach his Word to his people. God also often grants his people a second chance, even after he has acted in judgment on them. Such renewed opportunity cannot be taken casually but requires a renewed commitment to live according to God's Word.

Takeaway

How different God's people would be if all believers committed themselves, as Ezra did, "to study the law of the LORD, obey it, and teach its statutes and ordinances" (7:10)! Knowing what God says is important—and this is found only in his holy Word. But knowing alone is not enough. Doing or obeying is necessary. Discipling others then follows as a natural outgrowth of one's own spiritual learning and transformation.

NEHEMIAH

Author

The book is named for Nehemiah, the leading character (1:1). Jewish tradition, however, ascribed the final compilation to Ezra.

Date

Around 430 BC, after the final group of Jewish exiles returned from Babylon in 445 BC under Nehemiah. Ezra-Nehemiah originally was one book that was divided into two books in the fourth century AD.

Big Picture

Through Nehemiah's leadership God enabled the Israelites to rebuild and dedicate Jerusalem's walls as well as to renew their commitment to God as his covenant people.

Summary

Nehemiah held the distinguished position of cupbearer to Artaxerxes, the king of Persia (1:11). Visitors informed Nehemiah that Jerusalem's walls remained broken down. Nehemiah requested permission to go to Jerusalem and see the situation firsthand. Nehemiah's first act in Jerusalem in 445 BC was to inspect the walls at night (2:15). He then called an assembly and convinced the people of the need for a building program. After facing trouble from outside enemies (chap. 4) and internal tensions from the Israelites themselves (chap. 5), the city wall was rebuilt in 52 days (6:15). Nehemiah, along with his colleague Ezra, then led a great revival among the people (chaps. 8–10). Nehemiah returned to Persia but later returned to Jerusalem in 432 BC to serve a second term as governor, during which time he continued to lead the people in renewed commitment to the Lord (chaps. 12–13).

Key Verses

"If it pleases the king, and if your servant has found favor with you, send me to Judah and to the city where my ancestors are buried, so that I may rebuild it" (Neh 2:5).

"The wall was completed in fifty-two days, on the twenty-fifth day of the month Elul" (Neh 6:15).

Food for Thought

Nehemiah was a key leader in the restoration of God's people from Babylon to Jerusalem. He called for undivided loyalty to the work at hand in the same way Jesus did when he said, "No one who puts his hand to the plow and looks back is fit for the kingdom of God" (Luke 9:62). Total commitment and undivided loyalty are key aspects of Christian discipleship that all believers' lives should demonstrate.

Takeaway

Distraction from the Lord's work is always a real danger. Recognizing this great peril and determining not to allow oneself to become sidetracked but resolving to remain singularly focused on the Lord's work is a mark of true discipleship.

ESTHER

Author

The book is named for Esther, the leading character. The author is unknown, but Jewish tradition identifies Mordecai as the writer.

Date

Written around 465 BC, the events in Esther occurred in Persia between Ezra 6 and 7 during the years 485–465 BC.

Big Picture

Esther, a Jewish beauty selected by the Persian king Ahasuerus (Xerxes I) to become his new queen, saved the Jews from Haman's wicked plot, so her relative Mordecai established the yearly Jewish feast of Purim.

Summary

The story centers in Susa (Shushan), the winter resort of Persian kings. Esther, a beautiful young Jewish woman, was selected to replace the queen. She was related to Mordecai, who earlier had uncovered a plot to kill King Ahasuerus. Haman, prime minister of Persia, was infuriated by Mordecai's refusal to bow to him. So Haman began to plot against Mordecai and all of the Jews. Haman had the Persian monarch sign a decree for the destruction of the Jews. Mordecai called on Esther to approach the king. He told Esther that God had placed her in her position for such a time as this. Esther risked her life and exposed Haman's plot to the king. Haman was executed, and the king issued an edict that the Jews could defend themselves against those hostile to them—which they did. An annual feast called Purim was established to commemorate and celebrate the Jews' deliverance.

Key Verses

"Who knows, perhaps you have come to your royal position for such a time as this" (Esth 4:14).

"I will go to the king even if it is against the law. If I perish, I perish" (Esth 4:16).

Food for Thought

The book of Esther is famous in part because it does not directly mention God. Yet one cannot understand the story apart from God's remarkable presence and providence with his people—however invisible he may seem to be at times. God's providential care over believers committed to him in the midst of overwhelming challenges to their faith is his responsibility. Our duty is to take a stand for him whether we perish for doing so.

Takeaway

Sometimes God places people in positions in which they later can do great good for his plan and his people, even though the reason they are in such a position may not be clear initially. Sacrificing one's own needs for the good of others is one way believers show they are following the example of Jesus.

THE BOOKS OF POETRY
AND WISDOM

Traditionally, we speak of Psalms and Song of Songs as being the books of biblical poetry and Job, Proverbs, and Ecclesiastes as biblical wisdom.

The psalms express every emotion the believer encounters in life, be it praise and love for God, anger at those who practice violence and deceit, personal grief and confusion, or appreciation for God's truth. Song of Songs celebrates the joy of love between man and woman.

We can succinctly summarize the three books of Wisdom literature as follows. Proverbs teaches the basic principles of wisdom. It addresses the young man on the brink of making decisions that will follow him all his life. It describes unchanging principles for living a wholesome and honorable life. The book of Job contemplates the problems of the uneven distribution of suffering and success in the world. How is it that we see so many examples of immoral people thriving and prospering, while others who, are surely no worse and are often much better, suffer miserable lives of deprivation? The book of Job wrestles with this by considering the case of a man whom God afflicted not because of his sin but because of his righteousness. Ecclesiastes reflects on the brevity and apparent insignificance of human life. Against the certainty of death and the passing of time, it considers all of the standard human achievements—wisdom, wealth, and power—to be meaningless. Neither book tells us explicitly what God's hidden purpose is, but both assert that even if we remain in the dark about what God is doing, we can still show ourselves wise by fearing him and turning from evil (Job 28:28; Eccl 12:13).

Old Testament poetic and wisdom literature evidence a number of features. Some of the most common are *parallelism,* a device in which one line of poetry is followed by a second that in some way reiterates or reinforces the first. Several types of parallelism are found. In *synonymous parallelism* the second line says the same thing in the same word order as the first line; only the vocabulary differs. In *antithetic parallelism* the second line often reinforces the first by stating the same thought from a negative perspective. With *synthetic parallelism* the second line is not actually parallel to the first, but it reinforces the idea expressed by adding a reason or explanation. Another characteristic is *chiasm,* a literary device in which the second line mirrors and thus reinforces the first by reversing the sequence of words or phrases. Other literary patterns are also found. *Numeric proverbs* enumerate a number of items or occurrences that share a common characteristic. In an *acrostic poem* each line or section begins with a successive letter of the Hebrew alphabet. *Rhetorical devices* designed to make biblical poetry and wisdom easy to remember also are found. Hebrew poems contain rhyme, alliteration (repetition of initial sounds), and even puns. Simile, a comparison using *like* or *as,* also occurs frequently. One can find sarcastic humor as well as paradox, a statement contrary to common sense that is nevertheless true.

Biblical poetry and wisdom are at the same time both great literature and the eternal Word of God. This literature intrigues and delights us even as it rebukes and instructs.

JOB

Author

The book is named for Job, the leading character. The author is unknown.

Date

The book could have been penned any time between Moses and the end of the Old Testament (1400–400 BC), but perhaps it was composed around 950 BC during Solomon's reign, even though its setting seems to be in the patriarchal period.

Big Picture

After the upright Job suddenly lost family, health, and possessions, he and his friends dialogued at length about the reasons for his sufferings. God alone had the final word and ultimately restored Job's losses.

Summary

The prologue to the book of Job (chaps. 1–2) describes the setting for the ensuing drama. Job was a wealthy man of perfect integrity. Satan challenged Job's motivation for his commitment to God; and, unbeknown to Job, the Lord allowed Satan to test Job. In three cycles of speeches (chaps. 4–27) Job's friends reminded him that God blesses the upright and punishes the wicked. They urged Job to examine his life and confess his hidden faults. In four speeches (chaps. 32–37), Elihu, a younger man, admonished Job in the same manner. Then the Lord spoke and overwhelmed Job with his majesty and power and silenced Job's friends (chaps. 38–41).

In the end the epilogue (42:7-17) shows the Lord restored Job and his fortunes.

Key Verses

"Naked I came from my mother's womb, and naked I will leave this life. The LORD gives, and the LORD takes away. Blessed be the name of the LORD" (Job 1:21).

"Anyone born of woman is short of days and full of trouble" (Job 14:1).

"I had heard reports about you, but now my eyes have seen you. Therefore, I reject my words and am sorry for them; I am dust and ashes" (Job 42:5-6).

Food for Thought

God receives glory even when his people suffer and persevere in faith without understanding why. From a merely human point of view, the answer is that there is no answer given to the problem of evil. From a divine perspective the answer is that God's glory is served even when evil is permitted— Christ's suffering and death are a prime example of such.

Takeaway

Like Job, sometimes we have no idea why suffering and evil have befallen us or why bad things happen to good people. Nevertheless, we are in no position to challenge God and his wisdom. Our response should be to continue to trust the Lord and his loving care for his own, knowing that we may have to wait until eternity for everything to be made clear.

PSALMS

Author

David is mentioned in the titles of 73 psalms. Twelve psalms are ascribed to Asaph and 10 to "the sons of Korah." Other named authors are Moses, Solomon, Heman, and Ethan. Fifty psalms are anonymous, although Jewish tradition assigns some of these to Ezra.

Date

The oldest psalm, Psalm 90, is that of Moses (1400s BC). The largest group was composed during the Davidic era (1010–970 BC). The final compilation probably occurred during the time of Ezra and Nehemiah (458–430 BC). Psalm 137 may have been the last psalm composed.

Big Picture

God, the true and glorious King, is worthy of all praise, thanksgiving, and confidence—whatever the occasion in personal or community life.

Summary

The book of Psalms is subdivided into five smaller books— Psalms 1–41, Psalms 42–72, Psalms 73–89, Psalms 90–106, and Psalms 107–150—each ending with a doxology. The Psalter contains hymns, laments, songs of thanksgiving, royal psalms, enthronement psalms, penitential psalms, and wisdom psalms. Nine psalms are alphabetical, being built on successive letters of the Hebrew alphabet. A number of psalms are messianic and look to the New Testament for their fulfillment in the life and death of Jesus. Psalm 1 sets the tone for the whole Psalter by presenting two ways of life and the outcome of each. Psalm 23 contains some of the most recognized words from the Bible and presents the Lord as the Shepherd who provides, guides, and cares for his sheep. Psalm 51 is a psalm of forgiveness and cleansing after falling into sin. In Psalm 119, the longest psalm, almost every verse contains a reference to God's Word.

Key Verses

"The LORD is my shepherd; I have what I need" (Ps 23:1).

"Let everything that breathes praise the LORD. Hallelujah!" (Ps 150:6).

Food for Thought

The Psalter in its final form was designed as "The Hymnal of Second-Temple Judaism." The purpose of the individual poems as well as the entire collection process for the Psalter was to preserve the inspired words of Israel's songwriters as they expressed the heights and depths of their relationship with God. The poems were preserved to guide God's people in later times in how to approach him no matter what experiences they were undergoing. Above all, the psalms were meant to be sung to God as expressions of delight in him.

Takeaway

The psalms, which were meant to be sung, are a timeless resource for the people of God in their worship of the living God; as such, they provide a good pattern for believers to begin to do so.

PROVERBS

Author

Primarily Solomon, but Agur (chap. 30) and King Lemuel (chap. 31) also are named along with anonymous wise men who wrote the proverbs collected in 22:17–24:34.

Date

Between 950 and 700 BC.

Big Picture

Those who follow God's wise design for living avoid the perils that others fall into and enjoy life on earth as God meant it to be lived.

Summary

The beginning and end of wisdom are to fear God and avoid evil (1:7; 8:13; 9:10; 15:33). The world is a battleground between wisdom and folly, righteousness and wickedness, good and evil. This conflict is personified in Lady Wisdom (1:20-33; 4:5-9; 8; 9:1-6) and Harlot Folly (5:1-6; 6:23-35; 7:6-27; 9:13-18). Both "women" offer love and invite simple young men to their homes to sample their wares. Wisdom's invitation is to life (8:34-36); the seduction of Folly leads to death (5:3-6; 7:22-27; 9:18). After Proverbs 1–9 have introduced this divinely inspired worldview and laid out its main themes, the short sayings of Proverbs 10–31 are then to be understood in light of the first nine chapters.

Key Verses

"The fear of the LORD is the beginning of knowledge; fools despise wisdom and discipline" (Prov 1:7).

"Trust in the LORD with all your heart, and do not rely on your own understanding; in all your ways know him, and he will make your paths straight" (Prov 3:5-6).

Food for Thought

Proverbs shows that humans may live by a right way or a wrong way, a wise way or a foolish way. The right way is not the easy way, but those who live by it find great reward. All of life's relationships may be governed by the wise teachings of this book.

Takeaway

True wisdom goes beyond theoretical knowledge into practical guidelines for facing life's challenging issues successfully: true wisdom is to live according to God's way—his instruction—and allow his Word to penetrate one's thinking, values, and actions.

ECCLESIASTES

Author

Traditionally ascribed to Solomon.

Date

Around 935 BC.

Big Picture

Although human beings can accumulate many things, accomplish much, and achieve great wisdom, these are without profit and ultimately pointless unless one has lived in fear and obedience to God.

Summary

Ecclesiastes shows us that we must not waste our lives in pursuits that in the light of death ultimately mean nothing. The book warns about the pursuit of intellectual accomplishments (1:12-18; 2:12-17; 6:10–7:6; 7:11-29). Ultimately, the wise person and his works, like the fool and his deeds, perish. The book also warns against wealth and luxury (2:1-11,18-26; 4:4-8; 5:10–6:9; 7:11-14; 10:18-20; 11:1-6). Those who pursue riches waste their lives in anxiety and toil. Wealth of itself is a fraudulent substitute for true contentment. Likewise, political power is inherently corrupting, and the worst evils in the world are committed by cruel or incompetent people with power (3:15-17; 4:1-3,13-16; 5:8-9; 7:7-10; 8:1–9:6; 9:13–10:20). Irrational zeal and excess for religion also come in for criticism in Ecclesiastes (5:1-7; 7:15-29). Ecclesiastes recommends that we enjoy life and fear God, remembering that he is our Judge (12:8-14).

Key Verses

"'Absolute futility,' says the Teacher. 'Absolute futility. Everything is futile'" (Eccl 1:2).

"So remember your Creator in the days of your youth: Before the days of adversity come, and the years approach when you will say, 'I have no delight in them'" (Eccl 12:1).

Food for Thought

Ecclesiastes answers the question, What is the meaning of life? The author showed at length the failure of the answers offered by those who live life "under the sun," that is, apart from God's revealed truth. Materialists seek to find life's object in the abundance of possessions or achievements. Sensualists seek to discover meaning in physical pleasure (food, sex, excitement, adventure). Scholars seek to find purpose through intellectual inquiry (wisdom). All those attempts are futile, absolute futility, utterly meaningless (12:8). Life's meaning cannot be *discovered*; it is only *revealed* by God.

Takeaway

How we live our lives is of eternal significance; so even though we are capable of accomplishing many wonderful things in this life, our primary focus should be on God's revelation and eternity—for they are what define the true meaning and lasting outcome of life.

SONG OF SONGS

Author
Solomon (1:1).

Date
Around 965 BC.

Big Picture
A bride and groom—then wife and husband—celebrate with exuberant passion God's wonderful gift of the love they share by describing the intimate dimensions of their love—physical, emotional, and spiritual.

Summary
The Song of Songs is a celebration of the goodness and beauty of romantic love between a husband and wife. Several speakers appear in the love song—a woman, a man, a chorus of young women from Jerusalem, a narrator, and the woman's brothers. In the Song we see a return to paradise in a courtship that blossomed in the uncluttered beauty of nature (1:15–2:3; 2:8-14), in a wedding night consummated with allusions to the garden of paradise (4:12–5:1), and in a marriage that delights in innocent lovemaking (4:1–5:1; 7:1–8:3). The Song's last praise of love captures all of this (8:5-7) as it compares the power of romantic love to the eternal fire of God that no waters or rivers can quench.

Key Verses
"I am my love's and my love is mine" (Song 6:3).

"A huge torrent cannot extinguish love; rivers cannot sweep it away" (Song 8:7).

Food for Thought

The Song of Songs explores the question, Should a husband and wife enjoy the amorous and erotic dimension of their relationship? The answer is, yes indeed! Although people often abuse or distort erotic love, it is a wondrous and normal part of marriage to be savored as God's gift. It is not claiming too much to call this book "The Bible's Romance Manual for Marriage."

Takeaway

Married couples are to enjoy to the full the sexual dimension of their relationship. For those thus bound in this exclusive and binding marital union (7:10), human bodies are not evil, sex is not dirty, physical desire and sensual pleasure need not be suppressed or repressed. God designed human beings to appreciate all these and to enjoy the pleasures that come from them.

THE OLD TESTAMENT PROPHETS

What are the Old Testament Prophetic Books? First, they are the books written by or containing the messages of ancient Israel's "writing prophets" (as opposed to prophets such as Elijah and Elisha who had important ministries but left no written books themselves). The Prophetic Books traditionally are divided into the "Major Prophets" and the "Minor Prophets." The Major Prophets included Isaiah, Jeremiah, Ezekiel, and sometimes Daniel. The "Minor Prophets" were so named not because of their lesser importance but their length—they are significantly shorter than the longer books of the Major Prophets. The twelve Minor Prophets came to be known in Jewish tradition as "the Twelve" or "the Book of the Twelve."

The Prophetic Books may be characterized by style and function. First, they employ an elevated rhetorical style that often takes the form of poetry. Second, they present their

messages as received directly from God (as seen in their opening verses). Third, they use an inventory of literary forms such
as lawsuit, lament, woe, and promise. And fourth, because of
the common function of the prophets as "enforcers" or "pros-
ecutors" of God's covenant, these books call for behavioral
changes on the part of the disobedient covenant people.

This focus on behavioral change explains the prophets'
use of messages of indictment, instruction, judgment, and
hope or salvation. Indictment messages identified Israel's sins
and God's attitude toward them. Instruction told them what
they must do about it, and judgment and hope messages motivated the listeners to obey by explaining the consequences of
disobedience (judgment) or of repentance and faith (hope).

For many people today the word *prophecy* has only one
association—predictive prophecy. But it would be inaccurate
to think of the prophets as mere predictors of the future.
Students of the prophets who concentrate on prophetic fulfillment to the neglect of the rest of the prophet's message
miss the particular historical circumstances that called for
a prophetic word from the Lord. Recognizing the nature of
the Prophetic Books as behavioral exhortation has important
implications.

ISAIAH

Author

Isaiah, son of Amoz (1:1).

Date

Around 680 BC.

Big Picture

Isaiah prophesied that because of continued idolatry God would send Judah into Babylonian captivity, yet he would graciously restore them through the work of his Servant who would bear away their sins by his death.

Summary

Isaiah's book is divided into two major sections, "The Book of Judgment" (chaps. 1–39) and "The Book of Comfort" (chaps. 40–66). The first part of the book (chaps. 1–39) emphasizes sin, the call to repentance, and judgment; the second part (chaps. 40–66) emphasizes the hope of restoration. In the first part of the book, Assyria is the menace. The northern kingdom eventually would fall to the Assyrians, and the Assyrians would then threaten the southern kingdom. Isaiah encouraged Judah's kings not to trust in political alliances with Assyria, Egypt, or the Babylonians but to trust in the Lord. In the second part of the book (chaps. 40–66), the Jews held captive in Babylon are the focus of Isaiah's words of comfort, conciliation, and restoration.

Key Verses

"Holy, holy, holy is the LORD of Armies; his glory fills the whole earth" (Isa 6:3).

"For a child will be born for us, a son will be given to us, and the government will be on his shoulders. He will be named Wonderful Counselor, Mighty God, Eternal Father, Prince of Peace" (Isa 9:6).

"The grass withers, the flowers fade, but the word of our God remains forever" (Isa 40:8).

Food for Thought

Perhaps more than any other part of Isaiah, the passages describing a future anointed king (the Messiah; 9:1-7; 11:1-9) and those describing the Servant (42:1-9; 49:1-6; 50:4-6; 52:13–53:12) have attracted the interest of Christian readers of the book. From the time of the New Testament, Christian readers have understood Jesus Christ as the ultimate fulfillment of the expectation of a future king and suffering servant who delivers his people through his death for their sins.

Takeaway

Since the New Testament writers quoted Isaiah more than any other book of the Old Testament, believers should freely quote Isaiah's messianic passages to support and clarify New Testament truth when they present the redemptive message of the gospel.

JEREMIAH

Author

Jeremiah, the son of Hilkiah (1:1).

Date

Around 586 BC.

Big Picture

Jeremiah's main message was that Judah had fallen under the curse of God and was doomed to Babylonian exile because of its refusal to turn from sin; nevertheless, he prophesied that the exile would be limited, that Babylon would fall, and that God's gracious salvation through a new covenant lay on the other side of divine wrath.

Summary

The book begins with Jeremiah's call and commission as a young man (chap. 1). This is followed by chapters 2–24, which focus on Jeremiah and his people. Jeremiah's basic message, for which he suffered humiliation and persecution, was God's inevitable and inescapable judgment on Judah because of its sin and rebellion. Chapters 25–51 focus on Jeremiah's prophecies against the Gentile nations. The book closes with a historical appendix on the fall of Jerusalem and its aftermath in chapter 52. Perhaps the two best known prophecies of Jeremiah's 40-year ministry are his temple sermon, in which he condemned those who believed God would not bring judgment on them because they possessed the temple (chaps. 7–10; 26), and his prophecy of a new covenant (chaps. 30–33) that would be written on the hearts of God's people (31:31-34).

Key Verses

"See, I have appointed you today over nations and kingdoms to uproot and tear down, to destroy and demolish, to build and plant" (Jer 1:10).

"'This is the covenant I will make with the house of Israel after those days'—the LORD's declaration. 'I will put my teaching within them and write it on their hearts. I will be their God, and they will be my people'" (Jer 31:33).

Food for Thought

Jeremiah was the prophet of "the word of the LORD" (1:2). Jeremiah proclaimed, "This is the LORD's declaration" 157 times. But this prophetic word Jeremiah spoke was more than an objective revelation from God to the nation. God's words were to be joy and food for Jeremiah's own soul (15:16). However, God's word was sometimes a burden to the prophet. He sometimes grew tired of bringing God's message of judgment to an unresponsive people. Nevertheless, despite threats, discouragement, persecution, and rejection, Jeremiah remained faithful to his commission to the end.

Takeaway

As heralds of God's message, our responsibility is to be faithful to our calling to proclaim God's Word to all people, warning them of judgment and offering the hope of redemption and renewal, no matter how they respond to us or to the Word of the Lord.

LAMENTATIONS

Author

Unknown; tradition assigns the book to Jeremiah.

Date

Soon after the destruction of Jerusalem and its temple in 586 BC.

Big Picture

A skillful and emotional poet described the devastation of the city of Jerusalem and its temple—brought by the Babylonian army but ultimately caused by the Lord's anger against his people—and poured out his own personal expressions of sorrow.

Summary

The laments in Lamentations 1–4 are alphabetical acrostics, following the 22 letters of the Hebrew alphabet. These lamentations express the emotions of the poet over the fall of Jerusalem. The fact that there is an uneven number of poems allows the middle poem (chap. 3) to be the midpoint of the book. Accordingly, the first two chapters form the steps leading up to the climax of 3:22-24, and from that point there is a descent in chapters 4 and 5. Chapters 1 and 5 are overall summaries of the disaster, chapters 2 and 4 are more detailed descriptions of what took place, and chapter 3 occupies the central position. Throughout the laments it is acknowledged that Judah deserved its punishment, but along with this admission of guilt is a call for the punishment to end and a call for the enemies who carried it out to be punished in return (4:22).

Key Verses

"Is this nothing to you, all you who pass by? Look and see! Is there any pain like mine, which was dealt out to me, which the LORD made me suffer on the day of his burning anger?" (Lam 1:12).

"Because of the LORD's faithful love we do not perish, for his mercies never end. They are new every morning; great is your faithfulness!" (Lam 3:22-23).

Food for Thought

Rebellion against God cannot go on indefinitely. However, even when the punishment or loss is deserved, intense expressions of grief are a normal part of human experience. There is no joy in seeing God punish disobedient people, only sorrow. Times of intense suffering teach us to turn to God in prayer. Times of national catastrophe and personal disaster call for steadfast trust in God.

Takeaway

Whether we desire to see God rain down destruction on disobedient and rebellious people or we lament their loss indicates the extent to which we are aligned with God's own heart.

EZEKIEL

Author

Ezekiel, son of Buzi (1:3).

Date

Completed around 570 BC.

Big Picture

From exile in Babylon, Ezekiel's stunning visions and startling symbolic acts were prophecies for the Israelites to teach God's sovereign plan over them in the history of his kingdom, so that "they will know that I am the LORD" (6:10).

Summary

The book is built around the three "visions of God" (1:1; 8:3; 40:2) Ezekiel received. The first vision revealed God's glory (chaps. 1–3); the second God's judgment (chaps. 8–11); the third God's transformed people and temple (chaps. 40–48). Chapters 1–3 present Ezekiel's call and commission. Chapters 4–24 relate the judgment on Judah and the reasons for it. In these prophetic declarations Ezekiel demolished the four pillars on which the people had based their security— an immutable and unconditional covenant, eternal and unconditional title to the land, an irrevocable line of Davidic kings, and Jerusalem as the eternal dwelling place of God. Chapters 25–32 contain oracles against seven Gentile nations. Chapters 33–48 prophesy the restoration of Israel to the land, a restored Davidic kingship, and a new temple to which God's glory returns.

Key Verses

"As for you, son of man, I have made you a watchman for the house of Israel. When you hear a word from my mouth, give them a warning from me" (Ezek 33:7).

"I will give you a new heart and put a new spirit within you; I will remove your heart of stone and give you a heart of flesh. I will place my Spirit within you and cause you to follow my statutes and carefully observe my ordinances" (Ezek 36:26-27).

Food for Thought

God set Ezekiel as a "watchman" over Israel (3:16-21; 33:7-9). The watchman's responsibility was to warn the people of impending danger. If the watchman neglected his duty and danger fell, the victims' blood would be required of the watchman. But if the watchman warned the people and they refused to take heed to his message, then the responsibility fell on the people themselves; the watchman was released of responsibility. So it is for believers today. We are called to warn people of the coming judgment and announce that today is the day of salvation. Whether they take heed or not, if we sound the warning, we have fulfilled our duty.

Takeaway

To be right with God, moral reformation or turning over a new leaf is not enough. Only with a new heart and God's indwelling Spirit can anyone follow and obey God's Word.

DANIEL

Author

Technically, the book is anonymous, but much of it is recorded as the first-person memoirs of Daniel. Jesus affirmed Daniel's authorship (Matt 24:15).

Date

Final composition around 530 BC.

Big Picture

Daniel recounts key events firsthand that occurred during the Jewish captivity in Babylon and also shares visions about the future that God gave him.

Summary

Daniel's book divides into two parts. The first part, chapters 1–6, consists primarily of historical material relating well-known stories about Daniel and his friends' experiences in Babylon under Babylonian and Persian kings. The second division, chapters 7–12, primarily contains prophetic revelations related to the rise and fall of earthly empires and the establishment of God's future kingdom on earth.

Key Verses

"Daniel determined that he would not defile himself with the king's food or with the wine he drank" (Dan 1:8).

"In the days of those kings, the God of the heavens will set up a kingdom that will never be destroyed, and this kingdom will not be left to another people. It will crush all these kingdoms and bring them to an end, but will itself endure forever" (Dan 2:44).

"You have not glorified the God who holds your life-breath in his hand and who controls the whole course of your life" (Dan 5:23).

Food for Thought

Daniel and his friends modeled living as God's people in a pagan world. They identified areas in which their faith allowed them to make accommodations to the culture and areas in which it was impossible for them to do so and remain faithful to the Lord. Learning from their examples will help believers know how to live in today's neo-pagan society and under ungodly world dominion.

Takeaway

The kingdoms of this world, no matter how powerful or extensive they seem to be, are not permanent; only God's kingdom is everlasting. This realization helps believers focus on that which is eternal and not on that which is merely temporal.

HOSEA

Author
Hosea (1:1).

Date
Around 715 BC.

Big Picture
Hosea's marriage to an adulterous wife and the children she bore graphically demonstrated God's "marriage" to his spiritually adulterous people Israel, who must respond to his covenant love and repent or face severe judgment.

Summary
The two broad divisions of the book of Hosea focus on Hosea's marriage (chaps. 1–3) and Hosea's messages (chaps. 4–14). The first three chapters establish a parallel between the Lord and Hosea. Both were loving husbands of unfaithful wives. Hosea's marriage situation gave him prophetic insight into God's perspective on the northern kingdom of Israel. Hosea's messages in chapters 4–14 deliver accusations against Israel and calls to repent. Most of the oracles in chapters 4–13 are judgmental in nature; chapter 14 however ends the book on a hopeful note. The dominant theme of the book is love— God's unrelenting love for his wayward people and Israel's unreliable love for God.

Key Verses
"When the LORD first spoke to Hosea, he said this to him: Go and marry a woman of promiscuity, and have children

of promiscuity, for the land is committing blatant acts of promiscuity by abandoning the LORD" (Hos 1:2).

"I desire faithful love and not sacrifice, the knowledge of God rather than burnt offerings" (Hos 6:6).

Food for Thought

Hosea is one of the most autobiographical of the Prophetic Books in that the opening account of Hosea's own marriage and family form a vital part of his unique message. God's word of grace and his call to repent are dramatically portrayed and punctuated by Hosea's scorned but constant love for his wayward wife Gomer and by the odd names of his three children. Hosea's marriage to the promiscuous Gomer brought him much heartache, but rather than ministering in spite of personal sorrow, Hosea found that his troublesome marriage was the foundation stone of his ministry.

Takeaway

Often those who have been wounded most deeply can become God's most sensitive and faithful servants. A broken heart and deep hurt can be the starting point for a fruitful ministry.

JOEL

Author

Joel, son of Pethuel (1:1).

Date

Either 800 or 500 BC.

Big Picture

Joel proclaimed that the people of Judah should interpret a severe locust plague as a forerunner of "the day of the LORD" that is "terrible and dreadful" (2:11) and that would consume the pagan nations—but also unfaithful Judah unless the people repented.

Summary

The first part of the book of Joel (1:1–2:17) describes a terrible locust plague concluding with a plea for confession of sins. The second part (2:18–3:21) proclaims hope for the repentant people coupled with judgment upon their enemies. The people of Judah evidently assumed that the coming "day of the LORD" would involve God's judgment on the pagan nations and not on God's people. Joel proclaimed that this view was wrong. The people of Judah would be restored only after they had been judged and had repented of their sins.

Key Verses

"Blow the horn in Zion; sound the alarm on my holy mountain! Let all the residents of the land tremble, for the day of the LORD is coming; in fact, it is near" (Joel 2:1).

"After this I will pour out my Spirit on all humanity; then your sons and your daughters will prophesy, your old men will have dreams, and your young men will see visions" (Joel 2:28).

"Everyone who calls on the name of the LORD will be saved" (Joel 2:32).

Food for Thought

Joel understood the locust plague as a judgment from God and a harbinger of the day of the Lord (1:2-20, esp. v. 15). Then Joel announced that a worse judgment was coming through a human army (2:1-11). From this we learn that God's judgment not only can fall directly on his people but that God uses other people and nations to render his judgment, as well as nature itself (what we call natural disasters). All of these types of judgments are designed not only to punish but to make God known and reveal his righteousness.

Takeaway

Joel pointed to a time when the Spirit of God would be present upon all God's people (2:28-29). On the day of Pentecost, Peter proclaimed that the new day of Spirit-filled discipleship, foretold by Joel, had arrived (Acts 2:16-21).

AMOS

Author

Amos, a sheep breeder, herdsman, and tender of sycamore figs (1:1; 7:14).

Date

Around 750 BC.

Big Picture

Amos announced judgment on Israel for their failure to bind authentic religious experience with a social conscience during a time of great prosperity for many but a time of economic hardship for others; thus Amos warned that injustice, immortality, and idolatry would bring divine judgment in the form of exile.

Summary

Amos prophesied during a time of great prosperity and military success for both Israel and Judah. However there was a huge economic gap between the rich, who enjoyed enormous wealth, and farmers, who were reduced to poverty. The more affluent swooped in with loans that the poor could not repay and then reduced the debtors to slavery and seized their lands. After a brief introduction (1:1-2), Amos recorded seven oracles against Israel's neighbor nations (1:3–2:5). This is followed by five sermons that give a detailed account of God's displeasure with Israel (chaps. 3–6). The fourth section (chaps. 7–9) contains five visions of Amos that all pronounce God's judgment on Israel. The final section of the book is a prophecy of future restoration (9:11-15).

Key Verses

"Prepare to meet your God!" (Amos 4:12).

"Hate evil and love good; establish justice in the city gate" (Amos 5:15).

"Let justice flow like water, and righteousness, like an unfailing stream" (Amos 5:24).

Food for Thought

Amos declared about himself, "I was not a prophet or the son of a prophet; rather, I was a herdsman, and I took care of sycamore figs. But the LORD took me from following the flock and said to me, 'Go, prophesy to my people Israel'" (7:14-15). Amos was not formally trained for the ministry; he was a humble man of humble background. Yet the Lord called him and used him to deliver his message. The most important qualification for doing the Lord's work is not special training but a willingness to be used in his service and do what he says.

Takeaway

We must never conclude, either as individuals or as a nation, that material prosperity and political power are indications that God approves of our lifestyles.

OBADIAH

Author
Obadiah (v. 1).

Date
Around 585–550 BC.

Big Picture
God's wrath against Edom for its sins is the single concern of this brief book; Obadiah prophesied that God would destroy the nation of Edom because of its pride and violence, particularly in its looking down on Judah at the time of its misfortune.

Summary
Obadiah begins with a prophetic messenger formula indicating that God is behind the message. Verses 2-9 give the divine verdict. Addressing Edom, God promised to defeat those supermen and topple their mountain capital, which reflected their lofty self-conceit. Edom's allies would let them down, and neither their famed wisdom nor their warriors would be able to save them. The catalog of Edom's crimes (vv. 10-14) functions as the accusation that warranted God's verdict of punishment (vv. 15-18). A future blessing is said to be in store for Israel, and they will possess the land of Edom (vv. 19-21).

Key Verses
"How Esau will be pillaged, his hidden treasures searched out!" (Obad 6).

"For the day of the LORD is near, against all the nations. As you have done, it will be done to you; what you deserve will return on your own head" (Obad 15).

"There will be a deliverance on Mount Zion, and it will be holy" (Obad 17).

Food for Thought

Nations often depend on their geographical setting (vv. 3-5), diplomatic treaties (v. 7), and the counsel of their wisest men for their security (v. 8) instead of trusting in the true God. This is a mistake. As Edom's story shows, by depending on their own human understanding (vv. 3,8) and by believing in the loyalty of their human allies (v. 7), they were doubly deceived.

Takeaway

God is concerned with how nations act as nations toward other nations, with how a nation responds to another nation in times of its calamities and disasters, and he holds them accountable.

JONAH

Author

Jonah, son of Amittai (1:1), is the central character and probably the author of his story.

Date

Perhaps around 780 BC.

Big Picture

After Jonah's disobedience to God's command for him to preach in Nineveh, the capital of Assyria, resulted in his being swallowed by a big fish, he then obeyed God and preached in Nineveh. The results were that the entire city repented and turned to God.

Summary

The book divides into two halves, each of which opens with the Lord's command to go preach in Nineveh (1:1-2; 3:1-2). To avoid this divine assignment Jonah tried to get as far away from Nineveh as possible. But God sent a storm and then a great fish to turn Jonah around. Finally, Jonah arrived in the great city of Nineveh. After Jonah preached for only one day, the people humbly repented (chap. 3). Jonah was angry that God spared the Ninevites from destruction. Through an incident with a plant and a worm, the Lord chided Jonah for not caring about the salvation of the 120,000 people of Nineveh who had repented and trusted in the Lord (chap. 4). God's unanswered question that ends the book is meant to provoke readers to think about how God's mercy relates to "the nations"—especially to wicked and evil ones.

Key Verses

"The LORD appointed a great fish to swallow Jonah, and Jonah was in the belly of the fish three days and three nights" (Jonah 1:17).

"May I not care about the great city of Nineveh, which has more than a hundred and twenty thousand people who cannot distinguish between their right and their left, as well as many animals?" (Jonah 4:11).

Food for Thought

Jonah preached a message of repentance (3:4), but he did not want to see the people repent and be saved (4:1-4,9-11)! In fact, he was angry that the Lord was willing to save these people! Jonah was a mass of contradictions—a prophet known mainly for disobeying God, a preacher angry at the success of his ministry, a believer more concerned about "creature comforts" than about people dying without knowing the Lord.

Takeaway

The Lord desires the salvation of the lost more than his servants do, which means that his people should pray that they see all people as God sees them—in need of hearing his message of good news and responding to it in such a way that it results in their salvation.

MICAH

Author

Micah, the Moreshite (1:1).

Date

Around 700 BC.

Big Picture

Micah's main message was against Judah, who he said must repent of idolatry and injustice or else go into exile before eventually being restored to divine blessing under the Ruler from Bethlehem.

Summary

Micah falls into three sections: predictions of judgment (chaps. 1–3), predictions of restoration (chaps. 4–5), and pleas for repentance (chaps. 6–7). The destruction of the northern kingdom of Israel in 722 BC should have been a sign and a warning to Judah. It was a warning they did not heed. Micah grieved over the terrible calamity coming upon Judah for their rebellion. Juxtaposed to the message of corruption and doom is the message of glorious exaltation (chaps. 4–5). God was at work to turn humiliation into glorious victory through a Messianic ruler who came not from proud Jerusalem but from insignificant Bethlehem (5:2). In the final section Micah made clear that God's primary demand was for justice, mercy, and humble obedience. Micah told the righteous remnant they should look expectantly for the Lord's deliverance and a time when the Lord would cast their sins into the depth of the sea.

Key Verses

"Bethlehem Ephrathah, you are small among the clans of Judah; one will come from you to be ruler over Israel for me. His origin is from antiquity, from ancient times" (Mic 5:2).

"Mankind, he has told each of you what is good and what it is the LORD requires of you: to act justly, to love faithfulness, and to walk humbly with your God" (Mic 6:8).

Food for Thought

When moral and spiritual decay set in to such an extent that they affect the social order, no class or group of people is exempt from the corrupting influence—whether rulers, leaders, judges, priests, prophets, or the people themselves (3:1-12).

Takeaway

True worship cannot be separated from everyday practice. True religion and what is "good" before the Lord do not consist in religious rituals and outward forms of religion but in the spirit in which one lives and acts before others and before the Lord (6:6-8).

NAHUM

Author

Nahum, the Elkoshite (1:1).

Date

Perhaps around 650 BC.

Big Picture

Nahum prophesied that God would destroy Nineveh, the capital city of the Assyrian empire, because of its wickedness and violence, and it would never rise again.

Summary

The book of Nahum may conveniently be divided into three sections: Nineveh's destruction decreed (chap. 1), Nineveh's destruction described (chap. 2), and Nineveh's destruction deserved (chap. 3). Whereas Nineveh escaped God's judgment when the people repented at the preaching of Jonah, no such outcome would happen again. In chapter 1 the Lord is portrayed as a divine Warrior vanquishing the wicked (1:2-8). In chapter 2 Nahum is transported in a vision to Nineveh's watchtower, where he witnesses the combined armies of the Babylonians and Medes attacking, invading, and sacking the city. Chapter 3 begins with a funerary lament. Whereas before there was "no end to the treasure" and "abundance of every precious thing" (2:9), now there were "dead bodies without end" (3:3). Like other great ancient cities that trusted in their fortifications, the Lord reduced the once proud city to the ash heap of history.

Key Verses

"The LORD is slow to anger but great in power; the LORD will never leave the guilty unpunished" (Nah 1:3).

"The LORD is good, a stronghold in a day of distress; he cares for those who take refuge in him" (Nah 1:7).

Food for Thought

Human beings can achieve a great deal apart from God. The Assyrian civilization, of which Nineveh was the capital, was highly advanced economically and militarily. Nevertheless, the Assyrians were cruel and evil and thus an abomination to God. Nahum shows that God does not recognize as great or good any person or nation that measures success apart from obedience to him.

Takeaway

When we are tempted to believe God is lacking in compassion, we should recall his extraordinary patience and continual appeals with both his people Israel and with the Gentile nations.

HABAKKUK

Author

Habakkuk (1:1).

Date

Probably between 609 and 605 BC.

Big Picture

Habakkuk struggled with how to understand God's actions in history, especially his use of an unrighteous nation as the instrument of his justice. God's answer to Habakkuk's objection was that "the righteous one will live by his faith" (2:4).

Summary

The first two chapters of Habakkuk consist of a dialogue between the prophet and God. Habakkuk first complained of injustice in Judah (1:2-4). God responded by announcing that he was sending the Chaldeans to punish Judah (1:5-11). Habakkuk then complained about God's answer, arguing that it seemed unfair for God to use the more wicked Babylonians to punish the less wicked Judeans (1:12–2:1). God responded that the Babylonians were indeed arrogant and would ultimately be punished; nonetheless, God would use the Babylonians just as he had determined (2:2-20). The final chapter consists of a psalm in which Habakkuk reflected on this dialogue with God.

Key Verses

"The righteous one will live by his faith" (Hab 2:4).

"The earth will be filled with the knowledge of the LORD's glory, as the water covers the sea" (Hab 2:14).

"But the LORD is in his holy temple; let the whole earth be silent in his presence" (Hab 2:20).

Food for Thought

The righteous of all eras may ask questions similar to those Habakkuk asked. God's people today, as God's people then, will benefit from hearing God's replies to Habakkuk's questions: Why does evil seem to go unpunished for so long? Why does God sometimes reprove a lesser evil by sending a greater evil? God's answer is that the just live by faith, regardless of whether they have all the answers.

Takeaway

Steadfast, persevering trust in God for deliverance has always been the hallmark of God's people. Though we do not know the answers to all of life's questions, we are to make sure we have by faith received God's gift of eternal life.

ZEPHANIAH

Author

Zephaniah, son of Cushi (1:1).

Date

Sometime between 640 and 612 BC, perhaps about 625 BC.

Big Picture

Although Zephaniah prophesied coming judgment against the nations, his main message was against Judah, whose sins were so serious they would go into exile on "the day of the LORD"; later they would be restored to righteousness.

Summary

Zephaniah's book is divided into two main sections: judgment in the day of the Lord (1:1–3:8) and salvation in the day of the Lord (3:9-20). Zephaniah 3:8 is the pivotal transitional exhortation that looks both backward and forward between these two sections. In view of the impending destruction of the "day of the LORD" (1:7-18; 2:2-3), Zephaniah's primary purpose was to extend an urgent invitation. He urged the people of Judah to seek the Lord alone in righteousness and humility (2:1-3). Zephaniah's immediate purpose was to warn idolatrous Judah of the Lord's imminent judgment (1:4-13). His ultimate purpose was to call out a "remnant" from all nations (Judah, 2:7-9; Israel, 3:12-13; all nations, 3:9-10) to trust in the Lord because of the coming day of his judgment upon the earth (1:2-3,17-18).

Key Verses

"The great day of the LORD is near, near and rapidly approaching. Listen, the day of the LORD" (Zeph 1:14).

"Seek the LORD, all you humble of the earth, who carry out what he commands. Seek righteousness, seek humility" (Zeph 2:3).

"For I will then restore pure speech to the peoples so that all of them may call on the name of the LORD and serve him with a single purpose" (Zeph 3:9).

Food for Thought

Zephaniah shows the universal human tendency toward evil. He named all kinds of people—Jerusalemites, Philistines, Moabites, Assyrians, and Ethiopians—who alike were condemned because of their sins against God. Arrogance, oppression, and violence deserve God's judgment, no matter what persons or nations have committed them.

Takeaway

When we speak of God's coming judgment, our primary purpose should always be to encourage unrepentant people to come to know the Lord Jesus Christ as personal Savior.

HAGGAI

Author

Haggai (1:1).

Date

Shortly after 520 BC.

Big Picture

Haggai proclaimed to the Jewish people who had returned from the Babylonian captivity God's command to rebuild the temple in Jerusalem, giving God's promise that the glory of the second temple would exceed that of the first temple.

Summary

The book of Haggai contains four short confrontational speeches in chronological and dated order that identify ways the leaders and people in Jerusalem should change their theological thinking and behavior. There is a logical progression in the structure: people must glorify God (1:1-15), stay committed to God's plans (2:1-9), please God by living holy lives (2:10-19), and serve him faithfully (2:20-23). The first speech was a reprimand and call to rebuild the house of God (1:1-15). The second speech was a reminder of the Lord's presence and future glory of the temple (2:1-9). The third speech involved religious principles about holiness and uncleanness (2:10-19). And the fourth speech promised the restoration of the Davidic line (2:20-23).

Key Verses

"'Go up into the hills, bring down lumber, and build the house; and I will be pleased with it and be glorified,' says the LORD" (Hag 1:8).

"My house still lies in ruins, while each of you is busy with his own house" (Hag 1:9).

Food for Thought

People hinder the work of God not only by actively doing evil but also through inactivity and neglect concerning the things of God. If God's people are passive when they should be passionate about his work, God's work suffers. On the other hand, God's people can be moved to do great things for him when their leaders encourage them to do so and when the Lord rouses the spirit of his people (1:14).

Takeaway

Apathy and focusing only on the needs and creature comforts of one's own family can be great hindrances to God's work; thus all believers should examine the way they are living, identify what is most important to them, and then set new priorities that will please God (Matt 6:33).

ZECHARIAH

Author
Zechariah, son of Berechiah (1:1).

Date
Around 518 BC.

Big Picture
Through night visions and prophetic oracles, Zechariah predicted the welfare of Jerusalem as God's beloved holy city into which the true King—God's servant, the Branch—would enter riding a donkey.

Summary
Zechariah 1–8 deals with the rebuilding of the temple after the exile, the priesthood, and the future of Jerusalem. Chapters 9–14 deal mostly with the distant future and coming messianic kingdom. Zechariah organized his book around eight visions (1:7–6:8), four oracles (6:9–8:23), and two pronouncements (9:1–14:21). The main themes of the night visions are God's judgment of the nations, his election and future blessing of Jerusalem, the purification of the land, rebuilding the temple, and the leadership of Zerubbabel and Joshua. The four oracles form the central and most prominent section of the book. They describe a messianic prototype receiving the signs of his office. Zechariah is told to make royal crowns that are to be placed in the temple as a reminder of what God is going to do. The coming Messiah will be both King and Priest. The two final pronouncements deal with God's establishing his kingdom on earth.

Key Verses

"The LORD says this: 'I will return to Zion and live in Jerusalem. Then Jerusalem will be called the Faithful City; the mountain of the LORD of Armies will be called the Holy Mountain" (Zech 8:3).

"Rejoice greatly, Daughter Zion! Shout in triumph, Daughter Jerusalem! Look, your King is coming to you; he is righteous and victorious, humble and riding on a donkey, on a colt, the foal of a donkey" (Zech 9:9).

Food for Thought

The Gospels incorporate more passages from Zechariah than from any other prophet. In Zechariah we see foreshadowed Jesus's royal entrance into Jerusalem (9:9), his betrayal for thirty silver pieces (11:12), his role as Shepherd (13:7) and Branch (3:8; 6:12), and the piercing of Jesus's body (12:10; see John 19:34,37; Rev 1:7).

Takeaway

Though a day is coming when the Lord Jesus Christ will rule and reign as King of kings, in the meantime believers are to imitate his life as a humble servant when he came the first time.

MALACHI

Author
Malachi (1:1).

Date
Around 450 BC, not long before Ezra's return to Judah, or 420 BC, before Nehemiah's second term as governor of Judah.

Big Picture
Malachi rebuked God's people for specific violations of the covenant, such as laws concerning sacrifice, divorce, and tithes; but he also prophesied the coming of "the Messenger of the covenant" (3:1, Jesus) who will set all things right.

Summary
Malachi's prophesies were originally for the second or third generation of people in Judah after the return from the Babylonian captivity. The temple was functioning and the city was rebuilt, but people had become perfunctory in their worship and lifestyles. Malachi's message is communicated in three interrelated addresses (1:2–2:9; 2:10–3:6; 3:7–4:6). His message was essentially one of accusation: as God's messenger he charged the people with violations of the covenant and gave specific examples. In his indictments Malachi presented Judah's sins largely by quoting the people's own words, repeating their own thoughts, and describing their own attitudes (1:2,6-7,12-13; 2:14,17; 3:7-8,13-15). But he also looked ahead to a time of wonderful blessing.

Key Verses

"'My name will be great among the nations, from the rising of the sun to its setting. Incense and pure offerings will be presented in my name in every place because my name will be great among the nations,' says the LORD of Armies" (Mal 1:11).

"'See, I am going to send my messenger, and he will clear the way before me. Then the Lord you seek will suddenly come to his temple, the Messenger of the covenant you delight in—see, he is coming,' says the LORD of Armies" (Mal 3:1).

Food for Thought

Malachi spoke to the hearts of a troubled people whose circumstances of financial insecurity, religious skepticism, and personal disappointments were similar to those often experienced by God's people today. The book contains a message that must not be overlooked by those who wish to encounter God and his kingdom and to lead others to a similar encounter. We have a great, loving, and holy God, who has unchanging and glorious purposes for his people. Our God calls us to genuine worship, fidelity to himself and to one another, and to expectant faith in what he is doing and says he will do in this world and for his people.

Takeaway

Just as the people of Malachi's day were to live in faithful covenant relationships in preparation for the coming of the great Messenger of the covenant, so believers today are to remain faithful to the Lord and to other members of the new covenant community while being prepared for the Lord's second coming.

THE GOSPELS AND ACTS

The Gospels are not biographies. They record little about Jesus's early life, interactions with immediate family members, vocational training, or physical appearance. They concentrate almost exclusively on the three years of his ministry, and even then they focus mainly on the last week of his life.

Each Gospel exhibits a distinctive theological emphasis. Matthew's Gospel presents Jesus as the son of Abraham and son of David, showing Jesus to be the Messiah and King. Mark's Gospel presents Jesus as the "Son of God" (Mark 1:1) who wields unparalleled authority over nature, sickness, death, and even demons. Luke's Gospel presents Jesus as the perfect Son of Man who came to save people from their sin. John presents Jesus as the divine eternal Word who became man to give eternal life to those who believe in him.

Matthew, Mark, and Luke provide complementary accounts of Jesus's life. Matthew was one of the Twelve and thus witnessed many of the events he recorded. Mark, according to church tradition, relied on the testimony of Peter, the preeminent spokesman and member of the Twelve. Luke candidly acknowledges that he himself was not an eyewitness but drew on the accounts of eyewitnesses in compiling his Gospel (Luke 1:2). All three accounts are therefore based on eyewitness testimony.

Most likely John wrote his Gospel last, in the AD 80s or 90s, perhaps a full generation after the other Gospels had been completed. John's Gospel is different from the three other canonical Gospels. On the one hand, John leaves out many significant events and teachings found in Matthew, Mark, and Luke. On the other hand, John includes some important events and teachings not included in these other earlier accounts. John features Jesus's extended encounters with characters such as Nicodemus (3:1-9) and a Samaritan woman (4:1-42). He also includes accounts of seven striking "signs" of Jesus. Among the extended teaching portions included in John are the Bread of Life Discourse (chap. 6), the Good Shepherd Discourse (chap. 10), and the Farewell or Upper Room Discourse, which includes the discourse on the Vine and the Branches and Jesus's high-priestly prayer (chaps. 13–17).

Luke conceived of his Gospel and the book of Acts as a coherent two-part narrative, viewing Acts as the sequel to his Gospel that picked up where it left off. In his Gospel, Luke narrated the fulfillment of messianic prophecy in and through the life, death, and resurrection of Jesus. In the sequel, the book of Acts, Luke narrated the fulfillment of Jesus's mission as it is extended through the church's global, Spirit-empowered witness.

The Gospels and Acts thus lay the foundation for the remainder of the New Testament, which probes the implications of Jesus's coming, his vicarious death and resurrection, and his eventual return as King of kings and Lord of lords.

MATTHEW

Author

Technically anonymous, but early Christian tradition assigned this Gospel to the apostle Matthew.

Date

AD 55–65.

Big Picture

Jesus fulfilled the Old Testament prophecies about the coming Messiah, created the church, and commissioned his followers to tell others the good news.

Summary

Matthew divided his Gospel into three sections: introduction (1:1–4:16), body (4:17–16:20), and conclusion (16:21–28:20). He began by recounting events surrounding Jesus's birth (1:18–2:23) and then moved to Jesus's baptism and temptation (3:1–4:16), which prepared him for his three-year ministry of preaching, teaching, and healing (4:23). Perhaps no portion of Scripture is as well known as Jesus's Sermon on the Mount (chaps. 5–7). In chapters 8–10 Matthew recorded 10 miracles in which Jesus demonstrated his authority over disease, natural catastrophes, demons, and death. Matthew showed a variety of responses to Jesus's authority and recorded a series of Jesus's parables (chaps. 11–18). Chapters 19–25 mark the transition from Galilee to Jerusalem. Jesus triumphantly entered Jerusalem, cleansed the temple, and taught why he did what he did and who he was. In chapters 26–28 Matthew related the conspiracy that ended in Jesus's crucifixion, burial, and resurrection.

Key Verses

"Go, therefore, and make disciples of all nations, baptizing them in the name of the Father and of the Son and of the Holy Spirit, teaching them to observe everything I have commanded you. And remember, I am with you always, to the end of the age" (Matt 28:19-20).

Food for Thought

That Jesus told his followers to make disciples of all nations shows the inclusive nature of the gospel. Abraham, from whom Matthew traced Jesus's lineage (1:1-2), was told that he would bring a blessing to all nations (Gen 12:1-3). Matthew presents Jesus as the new Abraham, the founder of a new spiritual Israel consisting of all people who choose by faith to follow him. Throughout Christian history believers have sought to take the good news of salvation in Jesus to all peoples and nations. We call them missionaries. We call them witnesses. We call them obedient!

Takeaway

The Great Commission that concludes Matthew's Gospel (Matt 28:16-20) reminds us that since the Lord Jesus Christ died and rose again to bring salvation to all who believe, we are to do what we can to deliver this message to the whole world.

MARK

Author

Technically anonymous, but early Christian tradition assigned this Gospel to John Mark.

Date

AD 50–60.

Big Picture

In his life, death, and resurrection, Jesus fulfilled the prophecies and role of the suffering Servant of the Lord, notably through his death as "a ransom for many."

Summary

Mark's Gospel begins with a prologue (1:1-13), which is then followed by three major sections. The first (1:14–8:21) tells of Jesus's Galilean ministry. There Jesus healed and cast out demons and worked miracles. The second section (8:22–10:52) is transitional. Jesus began his journey that would take him to Jerusalem. This central section begins and ends with two accounts of Jesus giving sight to blind men. The final section (11:1–16:8) involves a week in Jerusalem. Mark devoted more attention to these final eight days of Jesus's earthly life than any of the other Gospel writers. From the time Jesus entered the city, he was at odds with the religious leaders, who quickly brought about his execution. A brief appendix (16:9-20) in which some of Jesus's appearances, his commissioning of his disciples, and his ascension are recorded is attached to the Gospel.

Key Verses

"The time is fulfilled, and the kingdom of God has come near. Repent and believe the good news!" (Mark 1:15).

"For even the Son of Man did not come to be served, but to serve, and to give his life as a ransom for many" (Mark 10:45).

Food for Thought

Mark identified his theme in the first verse: "The gospel of Jesus Christ, the Son of God." That Jesus is the divine Son of God is the major emphasis of his Gospel. God announced it at Jesus's baptism in 1:11. Demons and unclean spirits recognized and acknowledged it in 3:11 and 5:7. God reaffirmed it at the transfiguration in 9:7. Jesus taught it parabolically in 12:1-12, hinted at it in 13:32, and confessed it directly in 14:61-62. Finally, the Roman centurion confessed it openly and without qualification in 15:39. Thus Mark's purpose was to summon people to repent and respond in faith to the good news of Jesus Christ, the Messiah, the Son of God (1:1,15).

Takeaway

Mark emphasized Jesus's mighty acts and his role as Suffering Servant who calls followers to take up their own cross and follow him. People cannot remain neutral about Jesus. They have to decide either for him or against him.

LUKE

Author

Technically anonymous, but early Christian tradition assigned this Gospel to Luke.

Date

About AD 60–61.

Big Picture

Jesus not only lived and ministered as the perfect human, but he also died and rose to new life as the Savior for sinners.

Summary

Following his prologue, Luke narrates the birth announcements of John and Jesus, their births, and Jesus's own self-awareness at age 12 in the temple (1:5–2:52). The next section documents the ministry of John the Baptist, Jesus's baptism, his genealogy back to Adam, and his temptation in the wilderness (3:1–4:13). From 4:14 to 9:50 Luke turned to Jesus's 18-month public ministry in Galilee. The "travel narrative" in 9:51–19:44 contains much material unique to Luke as Jesus journeyed to Jerusalem for the final time. In the concluding section (19:45–24:53) Luke explained how Jesus died and why apparent defeat became victory.

Key Verses

"For the Son of Man has come to seek and to save the lost" (Luke 19:10).

"Then he said to them all, 'If anyone wants to follow after me, let him deny himself, take up his cross daily, and follow me" (Luke 9:23).

Food for Thought

Nearly 60 percent of the material in the Gospel of Luke is unique. Thus, there is a great deal that readers of Scripture would not know if the third Gospel were not in the Bible. Notable among the distinctive portions are much of the material in Luke 1–2 about the births of John the Baptist and Jesus; the only biblical material on Jesus's childhood and pre-ministry adult life (2:40-52); most of the "travelogue" section about Jesus's journey to Jerusalem (9:51–19:44), including the stories of the good Samaritan, the prodigal son, the rich man and Lazarus, and Jesus's encounter and visit with Zacchaeus; and quite a bit of fresh material in the postresurrection appearances, including the experience of two disciples on the Emmaus Road and the only description in the Gospels of Jesus's ascension into heaven (24:13-53).

Takeaway

Luke made clear that Jesus died unjustly; yet, in the face of injustice, God still worked his plan through Jesus's resurrection. This helps believers remember and then be encouraged by knowing that injustice is transcended in God's plans.

JOHN

Author

Technically anonymous, but early Christian tradition assigned this Gospel to John.

Date

About AD 80–90.

Big Picture

Jesus is the sign-working Son of God who gives eternal life on the basis of his death and resurrection to all who believe in him.

Summary

After a prologue (1:1-18), in which John presented Jesus as the eternal Word who became man, and a brief section explaining the role of John the Baptist in relation to Jesus (1:19-51), John's Gospel is divided into two main parts. In the first section (chaps. 2–11) the focus is on Jesus's ministry to the world and the seven signs he performed that served as authentication for his nature and mission. The second major section (chaps. 12–21) reveals Jesus's teaching to his disciples about his sacrificial death. In a Farewell Discourse (13:31–16:33) unique to John's Gospel, Jesus told his disciples about the coming helper, the Holy Spirit, and prayed a prayer for himself, his disciples, and all believers (chap. 17). John showed that Jesus died as the true Passover Lamb (19:14) and narrated several different resurrection appearances— including those when Thomas was present and when Peter was restored and commissioned (chaps. 20–21).

Key Verses

"In the beginning was the Word, and the Word was with God, and the Word was God" (John 1:1).

"The Word became flesh and dwelt among us. We observed his glory, the glory as the one and only Son from the Father, full of grace and truth" (John 1:14).

"For God loved the world in this way: He gave his one and only Son, so that everyone who believes in him will not perish but have eternal life" (John 3:16).

Food for Thought

John makes clear Jesus is the Logos, the Word of God who was with God and ever was God. Jesus is God in the flesh. Further, Jesus used the significant phrase "I am" seven times in John, claiming the personal name of God as his own and making remarkable claims about both his person and his work. We should not be surprised when the message of Christ's deity leads either to saving faith or to total rejection of his claims and the salvation he offers.

Takeaway

John explicitly stated his purpose for writing his Gospel near the end of his book—so that people would believe in Jesus and experience eternal life (20:30-31). Since that was John's purpose, we should use this Gospel to reach unbelievers with the gospel.

ACTS

Author

Luke, although the book of Acts technically is anonymous.

Date

Around AD 61–62.

Big Picture

Christianity spread from Jerusalem to Rome and from Jews to Gentiles by the power of the Holy Spirit, working especially through Peter and Paul.

Summary

The book of Acts provides a glimpse into the first three decades of the early church (about AD 30–63). Acts 1:8 provides the outline for the book. Chapters 1–2 relate the coming of the Spirit to the church. Chapters 3–5 focus on Jerusalem and the controversy between the apostles and the Jewish Sanhedrin. In chapters 6–8 the focus is on Stephen and Philip, two Hellenistic Jews, and their ministries. Chapters 9–12 complete the narrative of the church's witness in Jerusalem and Judea and relate the conversion of Paul and the beginning of the mission to the Gentiles by both Peter and Paul. Paul then led three missionary journeys, recorded in 13:1–21:16, taking the good news to Gentiles across the Mediterranean world. After returning to Jerusalem, Paul was arrested, imprisoned, faced a number of judicial hearings, eventually appealed to Caesar, and was sent as a prisoner to Rome to make that appeal (21:17–28:31).

Key Verses

"But you will receive power when the Holy Spirit has come on you, and you will be my witnesses in Jerusalem, in all Judea and Samaria, and to the end of the earth" (Acts 1:8).

"There is salvation in no one else, for there is no other name under heaven given to people by which we must be saved" (Acts 4:12).

Food for Thought

The book of Acts ties the other books of the New Testament together. It does so by first providing "the rest of the story" to the Gospels. The gospel and the message of the kingdom of God did not end with Jesus's ascension to heaven 40 days after his resurrection but continued on in the lives of his followers. Acts shows us how the words and promises of Jesus were carried out by the apostles and other believers through the power of the Holy Spirit. Second, the book of Acts gives us the context for much of the rest of the New Testament, especially the letters Paul wrote to the churches he had helped establish during his missionary journeys.

Takeaway

Depending on the Holy Spirit to empower them, believers should use whatever situations they find themselves in, even unpleasant ones, to tell others about Jesus and the salvation that is only available through him.

THE NEW TESTAMENT LETTERS

Twenty-one of the twenty-seven books of the New Testament are letters. In the first century letters (including most of those in the Bible) followed a well-known literary form that usually had four parts. First, a salutation or greeting from the sender to the recipients; second, a thanksgiving or prayer on behalf of the readers; third, the body or main part of the letter; and fourth, a farewell or closing.

How should one interpret the New Testament Letters? First, *read the Letters as historical documents*. Rather than first reading the New Testament Letters as written directly to the modern reader by God, the Letters should be read first as correspondence to churches in Italy, Greece, and Asia Minor that were facing specific challenges and threats nearly 2,000 years ago. The New Testament Letters certainly communicate God's revelation for modern readers, but before the modern reader can understand what God intends to say, he or she must first determine what the letter intended to communicate to the original readers. Readers who seek to interpret accurately the New Testament Letters should seek to understand the original historical context of each letter as fully as possible.

Second, *read the Letters as you would ordinarily read a letter.* Modern readers often read the New Testament Letters in a way that is different from how they read other letters. Few people receive a letter and read only a paragraph at a time or jump here and there, back and forth, to various portions of the letter. They recognize that if they are going to understand the letter, they must read it from start to finish. Yet many read the New Testament Letters haphazardly and, as a result, miss the progression and development of thought in the letter.

Third, *read the Letter with awareness of the important differences between then and now.* Sometimes statements in the New Testament Letters are culturally conditioned, meaning they were written assuming the conditions of first-century Jewish or Gentile culture in various parts of the ancient world. They may not apply to readers in a different culture or era in precisely the same way they applied to the original readers. Prudent application of texts that originally addressed cultural situations different from those of the modern reader requires *principalization.*

Principalization involves an attempt to discover the moral or theological principles that apply in all situations and that lie behind directives addressed to a situation different from today. Readers can discover such principles by asking: What instruction did the letter give to the original reader? What particular situation was the instruction addressing? How is my situation like that original situation? How is my situation different? If one's contemporary situation is similar to that of the original reader, the instruction may directly apply. However, if one's situation is different from that of the original reader, the instruction will still apply but less directly. Then the reader must identify the moral or theological principle that prompted the instruction and consider how that principle applies in his or her situation.

ROMANS

Author
Paul the apostle (1:1).

Date
Around AD 57.

Big Picture
Right standing with God is given freely to all those who have faith in Jesus Christ for salvation according to God's eternal plan.

Summary
God's righteousness is the theme of Romans (1:16-17). Both Gentiles (1:18–2:16) and Jews (2:17-29) have sinned and are in need of Christ's atoning work for their salvation (3:21-31). Paul demonstrated through the example of Abraham that God's way of justifying sinners is by faith (4:1-25). Those who trust in the redemptive work of God in Jesus receive his righteousness (chap. 5), are freed from the penalty and power of sin (chap. 6), but will still struggle with the reality of sin (chap. 7). In chapter 8 Paul described the believer's freedom from condemnation, futility, alienation from God, and eternal death by the power of the Spirit in his or her life. Paul then explained in chapters 9–11 that God was not finished with Israel. In the final chapters Paul taught that God's righteousness is to be expressed in the lives of believers within the family, the church, and the larger society (chaps. 12–16).

Key Verses

"For all have sinned and fall short of the glory of God" (Rom 3:23).

"For the wages of sin is death, but the gift of God is eternal life in Christ Jesus our Lord" (Rom 6:23).

"If you confess with your mouth, 'Jesus is Lord,' and believe in your heart that God raised him from the dead, you will be saved" (Rom 10:9).

Food for Thought

Salvation is comprehensive; it includes our past, present, and future. We once stood under God's condemnation, but Christ has saved us from the penalty of sins (justification); he is saving us from the power of sin (sanctification); and he will save us from the presence of sin (glorification).

Takeaway

Since all human beings fall short of God's perfect standard of righteousness, in order to be saved we must put our faith in the Lord Jesus Christ.

1 CORINTHIANS

Author

Paul the apostle (1:1).

Date

Around AD 55.

Big Picture

The many problems a congregation may have, whether doctrinal or practical, will be resolved as that church submits properly to the lordship of Christ and learns to love one another genuinely.

Summary

The church at Corinth was racked with many problems. Paul began this letter by dealing with the problem of those who bring division to the body of Christ (1:11–3:4). Paul next addressed a case of immorality in the church (chaps. 5–6). Then he answered the church's list of questions brought to him by a committee (see 16:12). Paul's recurring expression "now about" moves through a list of questions about males and females in marriage (7:1), virgins (7:25), food offered to idols (8:1), spiritual gifts (12:1), the collection for the believers in Jerusalem (16:1), and Apollos's future ministry (16:12). First Corinthians also contains the clearest exposition on the Lord's Supper (11:17-34) and on the resurrection (chap. 15). The "Love Chapter" (chap. 13) is the best known and most loved part of the letter.

Key Verses

"For the word of the cross is foolishness to those who are perishing, but it is the power of God to us who are being saved" (1 Cor 1:18).

"Now these three remain: faith, hope, and love—but the greatest of these is love" (1 Cor 13:13).

"I passed on to you as most important what I also received: that Christ died for our sins according to the Scriptures, that he was buried, that he was raised on the third day according to the Scriptures, and that he appeared" (1 Cor 15:3-5).

Food for Thought

First Corinthians contributes greatly to our understanding of the Christian life, ministry, and relationships by showing us how the members of the church—Christ's body—are to function together. Problems can arise in any church because the church is comprised of sinful, yet redeemed, people. Paul gave specific solutions to specific problems, but the underlying answer to all these problems is for the church and its members to live Christ-centered lives. It all comes down to living under the lordship and authority of Christ, the head of the church.

Takeaway

To build up one another as believers, we must demonstrate Christ's love in all of our relationships.

2 CORINTHIANS

Author
Paul the apostle (1:1).

Date
Around AD 56.

Big Picture
True Christian ministry, although it may have to be defended against false attacks, is commissioned by Christ and empowered by his Spirit.

Summary
After 1 Corinthians was not well received by the congregation, Paul paid the Corinthians a visit. False apostles led the Corinthians to disown Paul and his ministry. After leaving, Paul then wrote the congregation a now lost severe letter of stinging rebuke. With this, much of the congregation repented and reaccepted Paul's authority. Paul then wrote 2 Corinthians expressing his relief but still pleading with the unrepentant minority. Second Corinthians thus falls into two parts. In chapters 1–9 Paul expressed his joy that the majority had been restored to him and submitted to his apostolic authority. Chapters 10–13 are a blistering criticism of those who would not. In this section Paul defended his conduct, character, and call as an apostle and evangelist. Second Corinthians also contains the most extensive teaching in the Bible about the state of redeemed human beings between their death and the resurrection (5:1-8) and the most extensive New Testament teaching on Christian stewardship (chaps. 8–9).

Key Verses

"For we must all appear before the judgment seat of Christ, so that each may be repaid for what he has done in the body, whether good or evil" (2 Cor 5:10).

"But he said to me, 'My grace is sufficient for you, for my power is perfected in weakness.' Therefore, I will most gladly boast all the more about my weaknesses, so that Christ's power may reside in me" (2 Cor 12:9).

Food for Thought

Of all Paul's letters, this is the most personal and the most defensive. In it Paul mounted a defense of his apostolic authority and ministry.

Takeaway

When we are falsely accused, it is not wrong to defend ourselves, but when we do, we should always reflect the fruit of the Holy Spirit.

GALATIANS

Author
Paul the apostle (1:1).

Date
Around AD 49 or 52–55.

Big Picture
Sinners are justified and live a godly life by trusting in Jesus Christ alone, not by keeping the law or by counting on good works.

Summary
Paul wrote Galatians to clarify and defend "the truth of the gospel" (2:5,14). He did this by: (1) defending his message and authority as an apostle, (2) considering the Old Testament basis of the gospel message, and (3) demonstrating how the gospel message he preached worked practically in daily Christian living. Paul was astounded that so soon after his ministry among the Galatians they had defected from the gospel of grace. He went back to Abraham to show that the basis of right standing with God is faith (3:6-9). The purpose of the law was to convict people of sin and hold them captive until Christ was revealed (3:19–4:7). Paul then examined the nature of the liberty believers have through faith. While he rebuked the tendency toward legalism, he also deplored the opposite extreme of license (chap. 5). At the end of the letter, Paul summarized the issues of the entire letter in 6:11-18.

Key Verses

"Because we know that a person is not justified by the works of the law but by faith in Jesus Christ, even we ourselves have believed in Christ Jesus. This was so that we might be justified by faith in Christ and not by the works of the law, because by the works of the law no human being will be justified" (Gal 2:16).

"For you were called to be free, brothers and sisters; only don't use this freedom as an opportunity for the flesh, but serve one another through love" (Gal 5:13).

Food for Thought

Galatians has been labeled the "Magna Carta of Christian Liberty." Only the gospel gives true liberty. Paul told the Galatians, "For freedom, Christ set us free. Stand firm then and don't submit again to a yoke of slavery" (5:1). Such an exhortation is necessary because believers have a tendency to abandon their liberty in either of two directions—surrendering it to legalism or twisting it into a license to sin. Both are distortions of the gospel. True Christian liberty must be prized and protected because it cost so much—the death of our Savior and Lord who set us free.

Takeaway

Salvation is a gift of God's grace. It is unearned and undeserved and must be received by faith alone.

EPHESIANS

Author
Paul the apostle (1:1).

Date
About AD 61.

Big Picture
In God's eternal plan, God's great masterpiece the church has now been manifested, in which Christ is united with all the redeemed, whether Jew or Gentile, transforming relationships in this life and leading to a glorious future.

Summary
Ephesians divides into two parts: chapters 1–3 are doctrinal and chapters 4–6 are practical. There are no imperatives in chapters 1–3—everything is descriptive—but chapters 4–6 are filled with directives as to how believers are to conduct themselves in keeping with their calling. Paul first wanted his readers to have a fuller grasp of their salvation (1:3-14). He wanted them to know the power available to them through Christ (1:15-19), power that comes to persons who were dead in sin but saved by grace (2:1-10). In Christ both Jews and Gentiles are reconciled to God and to one another and are joined together in the church (2:11–3:21). In the second half of the letter, Paul turned to the application of redemption to the church, to personal life, and to family life. To conclude his letter Paul called on his readers to put on God's armor to avoid Satan's temptations and to triumph over his attacks (4:1–6:24).

Key Verses

"For you are saved by grace through faith, and this is not from yourselves; it is God's gift—not from works, so that no one can boast" (Eph 2:8-9).

"For he is our peace, who made both groups one and tore down the dividing wall of hostility" (Eph 2:14).

"Put on the full armor of God so that you can stand against the schemes of the devil" (Eph 6:11).

Food for Thought

Christ, through his death, brought peace between God and man and between Jews and Gentiles, two groups that were hostile to each other. These groups Christ united as one in the church, his body, of which he is the cornerstone and head.

Takeaway

Regardless of our different ethnic backgrounds, social status, gender, or race, when we become believers in Christ, we are to function as members of one family, the church.

PHILIPPIANS

Author
Paul the apostle (1:1).

Date
About AD 61.

Big Picture
Paul encouraged the believers at Philippi to embrace a spirit of unity and mutual concern by adopting the attitude of humility Jesus himself manifested.

Summary
Paul wrote to thank the church for a financial gift it recently had sent him in prison and to inform them of his circumstances and plans (2:19-30; 4:10-20). Seizing the opportunity, Paul exhorted the church (1:27–2:18) because heresy and disunity—spawned by false teachings (3:1-16) and personal conflicts (4:2-9)—threatened the church. In a hymn about Christ that dominates the epistle (2:5-11), Paul thus reminded the believers of who Jesus is and focused on his example of humility and self-sacrifice. Paul urged all the believers to adopt the same attitude as their Lord so they individually and collectively could live the Christian life vigorously and joyfully.

Key Verses
"Do nothing out of selfish ambition or conceit, but in humility consider others as more important than yourselves" (Phil 2:3).

"Adopt the same attitude as that of Christ Jesus" (Phil 2:5).

"Rejoice in the Lord always. I will say it again: Rejoice!" (Phil 4:4).

Food for Thought

Christian unity results when believers develop the mind of Christ. If believers will allow the outlook of Christ to guide their lives, harmony will be assured in the church and among its members.

Takeaway

Harmony, joy, and peace characterize the church that functions as it should.

COLOSSIANS

Author
Paul the apostle (1:1).

Date
About AD 61.

Big Picture
Jesus Christ is supreme over everything and thus is to have first place in the lives of believers.

Summary
The first part of Colossians (chaps. 1–2) is a polemic against false teachings. The second part (chaps. 3–4) is made up of exhortations to proper Christian living. Paul prayed that the Colossians would have a full knowledge and understanding of God's will and lead lives that were worthy of the Lord and pleasing to him. Paul then focused on the centrality of Christ, identifying him as the Creator of all things and head of the church, God in human form, and the agent of redemption and reconciliation. Paul attacked heretical views that failed to measure up to these truths. Paul next focused on the transformation Christ brings to believers' lives. He told his readers what they were to "put away"—all those practices that incur God's wrath—and what they were to "put on"—those things characteristic of God's chosen people, including how believers interact in their families and in other social structures.

Key Verses

"He is also the head of the body, the church; he is the beginning, the firstborn from the dead, so that he might come to have first place in everything" (Col 1:18).

"And whatever you do, in word or in deed, do everything in the name of the Lord Jesus, giving thanks to God the Father through him" (Col 3:17).

Food for Thought

A correct understanding of Christ is indissolubly linked to how believers live lives that are distinctive and reflective of the glory and grandeur of Christ. Only Scripture can give us such a correct understanding of our Savior and Lord.

Takeaway

Believers need to give up anything that denies Jesus his preeminent position as Lord in their lives, submitting to the rule of Christ in every area, for he is to have first place in everything.

1 THESSALONIANS

Author
Paul the apostle (1:1).

Date
About AD 50.

Big Picture
Whatever difficulties and sufferings believers experience in this life, the coming of Christ is the true hope of the Christian.

Summary
Paul dealt with four major topics in 1 Thessalonians, the first of which was his conduct in his ministry. In his absence critics had suggested that Paul operated out of ulterior motives (2:3-13). A second topic Paul addressed was persecution. Paul encouraged the believers not to be shaken by afflictions because Christians are certain to suffer (3:3-4). Sanctification was Paul's third topic. Salvation isn't finished once a person believes in Christ and receives forgiveness of sins. Paul's prayer for the believers was that God would establish their hearts "blameless in holiness" (3:13). Fourth, Paul focused on Jesus's return (4:13–5:11). Paul corrected some misunderstandings of this doctrine, assuring Christians they are not appointed to God's wrath. He also stated that Christians who are alive at Christ's return will be changed immediately and will meet Christ in the air without dying.

Key Verses

"May he make your hearts blameless in holiness before our God and Father at the coming of our Lord Jesus with all his saints" (1 Thess 3:13).

"For the Lord himself will descend from heaven with a shout, with the archangel's voice, and with the trumpet of God, and the dead in Christ will rise first. Then we who are still alive, who are left, will be caught up together with them in the clouds to meet the Lord in the air, and so we will always be with the Lord" (1 Thess 4:16-17).

Food for Thought

Just as people today want to know more about the end times, so did the Thessalonians. Knowing Christ will return, and perhaps at any time, should not be merely a matter of speculative information but a determining factor in how believers live their lives. Paul's prayer for the Thessalonians was, "May he make your hearts blameless in holiness before our God and Father at the coming of our Lord Jesus" (3:13). To be found living a life that pleases the Lord while waiting for his return should be every believer's desire and priority. Thus, for believers, what is to happen *then* determines how they live *now*.

Takeaway

Christ's return gives believers true hope; and since it could happen at any time, believers are always to be ready for the Lord's return.

2 THESSALONIANS

Author
Paul the apostle (1:1).

Date
About AD 50.

Big Picture
Whatever difficulties believers face, they should stand firm and continue living useful lives since Christ's return may not be until the distant future.

Summary
Paul commended the Thessalonians for their growing faith, maturing love, and patience in the face of persecution (1:3-5). God's people can be encouraged by knowing they will be vindicated when the Lord returns and will realize they have neither believed nor suffered in vain (1:6-12). However, with their focus on Jesus's second coming, some were wrongly teaching that the day of the Lord had already occurred. Paul reminded them that a full-scale rebellion must precede Christ's return and the "man of lawlessness" must first be revealed (2:1-12). He thus urged those who had stopped working to go back to work and provide for their own needs. Paul assured the Thessalonians of his prayers on their behalf and asked them to pray for him (3:1-18).

Key Verses
"In view of this, we always pray for you that our God will make you worthy of his calling, and by his power fulfill your

every desire to do good and your work produced by faith, so that the name of our Lord Jesus will be glorified by you, and you by him, according to the grace of our God and the Lord Jesus Christ" (2 Thess 1:11-12).

Food for Thought

The world is not getting better and better. Before Christ returns, there will be a great falling away from the faith, and the man of lawlessness empowered by Satan will make his appearance. Yet believers know that the darkest night only points to the coming of the golden day when Christ returns in glory.

Takeaway

No matter what happens, believers are to stand firm in their faith, hope, and love, always being ready for Christ's return.

1 TIMOTHY

Author
Paul the apostle (1:1).

Date
About AD 63.

Big Picture
Whatever challenges Christian leaders face in life and ministry, they are to make progress in holiness and help maintain order in congregational life.

Summary
Paul wrote to Timothy to encourage him in his growth as a Christian and as a church leader. Under the influence of two false teachers, some believers had moved away from sound doctrine and were more concerned with Jewish laws and rituals, myths, and speculation than about God's clear plan. Paul informed Timothy how such men should be dealt with (1:3-20; 4:1-16). Paul then instructed Timothy about prayer (2:1-7), the roles of men and women (2:8-15), the qualifications for those who aspire to church leadership (3:1-13), the care of widows (5:3-16), dealing with elders and criticisms about them (5:17-25), masters and slaves (6:1-2), and money (6:3-19). Paul closed his letter with a challenge to Timothy to fight a good fight as a soldier of God in his pursuit of holiness, in his persistence in service, and in protecting the truth of the gospel (6:11-21).

Key Verses

"An overseer, therefore, must be above reproach, the husband of one wife, self-controlled, sensible, respectable, hospitable, able to teach" (1 Tim 3:2).

"I have written so that you will know how people ought to conduct themselves in God's household, which is the church of the living God, the pillar and foundation of the truth" (1 Tim 3:15).

"Pay close attention to your life and your teaching; persevere in these things, for in doing this you will save both yourself and your hearers" (1 Tim 4:16).

Food for Thought

As the first of three New Testament letters Paul wrote to his younger gospel coworkers (1 and 2 Timothy, Titus), this book shows the importance of what one person can do for the Lord and his work. Timothy stands as an example of living one's life for the glory of God, for his work in the world and on behalf of his people, and for teaching others to do the same. Timothy's example also points to the importance of right doctrine and of God's people being a harmonious community of faith.

Takeaway

Leaders who are appointed to serve in shepherding roles in the church are to be selected based on the biblical criteria for measuring Christian maturity.

2 TIMOTHY

Author
Paul the apostle (1:1).

Date
About AD 66.

Big Picture
Christian leaders are to be unashamed of the gospel, carry on unwaveringly with the message about Christ entrusted to them, and faithfully transmit it to the next generation.

Summary
Second Timothy is Paul's last letter and his "last will and testament." Paul addressed the present (chaps. 1–2) and the future (chaps. 3–4). In the first section Paul admonished Timothy to keep the faith in the midst of suffering. He told Timothy to cultivate faithful followers to whom he could entrust the truth and who, in turn, would teach others. He also told Timothy to confront false teachers after making careful preparations to deal with them. In the second section Paul described an intensification of evil in the last days. He instructed Timothy to cling to the truth of the inspired Scriptures that he had learned and believed. Paul concluded his charge by stressing the need to preach God's Word. Timothy also needed to be prepared in any situation to speak a word of rebuke, correction, or encouragement; he was to do the work of an evangelist and fulfill his ministry (4:1-5).

Key Verses

"What you have heard from me in the presence of many witnesses, commit to faithful men who will be able to teach others also" (2 Tim 2:2).

"Be diligent to present yourself to God as one approved, a worker who doesn't need to be ashamed, correctly teaching the word of truth" (2 Tim 2:15).

"I have fought the good fight, I have finished the race, I have kept the faith" (2 Tim 4:7).

Food for Thought

Completing one's ministry faithfully to the end is admirable and should be the desire of every Christian leader. But this is not enough. There is more to a Christian leader's ministry than merely that which he does himself. Many Christian leaders never cultivate, train, and develop the next generation of leadership. Such failure is shortsighted. A faithful spiritual leader mentors potential leaders of the next generation who will be faithful to the gospel that has been entrusted to them and who will pass it on to leaders of the generation after them.

Takeaway

Spiritual leaders should mentor and develop a core of faithful men and women who can multiply their efforts—especially to the next generation.

TITUS

Author
Paul the apostle (1:1).

Date
About AD 63.

Big Picture
Whatever challenges they face in life and ministry, Christian leaders are to maintain order in their congregations, but only according to sound teaching.

Summary
Paul had left Titus on the island of Crete to appoint leaders in every town where there were believers. He set forth the qualifications for these elders because strong, godly leadership is vital in churches, especially when they are challenged by false teaching (1:5-9). Paul urged two approaches in contending with the false teaching. The first was verbal rebuke (1:13). The second was to teach sound doctrine (2:1). Such teaching accurately conveys God's revelation in Scripture and in Jesus Christ and moves to application in the details of people's lives. Paul articulated these applications for men, women, and slaves in light of what Christ has done and what he yet will do when he returns (2:2-14). Paul closed his letter by articulating the difference Christ makes in the lives of people, transforming them through his mercy and the work of the Holy Spirit (3:1-15).

Key Verses

"But you are to proclaim things consistent with sound teaching" (Titus 2:1).

"Make yourself an example of good works with integrity and dignity in your teaching" (Titus 2:7).

"Let our people learn to devote themselves to good works for pressing needs, so that they will not be unfruitful" (Titus 3:14).

Food for Thought

Many Christians do not like doctrine! They cringe when they hear the word. It conjures up images of dry, stale, petty arguments that few can understand. Such an image is unfortunate. Sound teaching is important to the Christian church and to the lives of believers. Sound teaching is important because much teaching is not sound. A lot of false teaching abounds in the world. Sound teaching is important because it leads to sound practice; it shows us how we should live our lives in the world and in our relationships with other believers.

Takeaway

Sound Christian teaching is the necessary foundation for everything worthwhile in the life of a congregation or an individual.

PHILEMON

Author
Paul the apostle (v. 1).

Date
About AD 61.

Big Picture
Everyone who has repented of sin and come to Christ should be welcomed as a brother or sister, treated gently, and forgiven by other believers for past wrongs committed.

Summary
Onesimus, a slave, had run away from his master, Philemon, and taken with him some of his master's money or possessions (vv. 15,18). He traveled to Rome where his path crossed Paul's, and he became a Christian (vv. 10,16) and a useful helper to Paul (v. 11). Philemon, Onesimus's master in Colossae, also had previously been converted through Paul's ministry (vv. 10,19) and had become Paul's "dear friend and coworker" (v. 1) and "partner" (v. 17) in the gospel service. Paul thus wrote to Philemon concerning Onesimus. Paul's clear preference was to keep Onesimus with him (v. 13), but Paul recognized that Philemon was Onesimus's legal owner and decided to send him back to Colossae (v. 12). Philemon could either reinstate Onesimus as a slave who was now also a Christian brother (vv. 15-16) or else set him free for further service to Paul back in Rome (vv. 13,20-21).

Key Verses

"For perhaps this is why he was separated from you for a brief time, so that you might get him back permanently, no longer as a slave, but more than a slave—as a dearly loved brother. He is especially so to me, but how much more to you, both in the flesh and in the Lord" (Phlm 15-16).

Food for Thought

The book of Philemon is open-ended. What did Philemon do? Did he beat Onesimus, which was his legal right, to make an example out of him before Philemon's other slaves? Did Philemon accept Onesimus as a Christian but nevertheless keep him as a slave? Did he set him free? We aren't told. What would you have done? Could you forgive and accept back into your trust, confidence, and household staff one who had stolen from you and done you such wrong?

Takeaway

The little book of Philemon is a powerful testimony to God's grace, the transforming power of the gospel, Christian love, forgiveness, and reconciliation.

HEBREWS

Author
Unknown.

Date
Perhaps around AD 66.

Big Picture
Jesus Christ, who is better than the angels, Moses, Joshua, and the Hebrew high priests, made a more excellent sacrifice and established a better covenant, ensuring that the old covenant is obsolete and that faith is a better way to live.

Summary
The first three verses define the theme of this book—Jesus Christ, God's Son, is God's supreme and final revelation and thus superior to all previous revelations. Jesus is presented as superior to angels because angels are created beings and he is eternal (1:4–2:18). Jesus is superior to Moses, who was merely a servant in God's household while Jesus is the Son in the house (chap. 3). Jesus is superior to Joshua, who only gave the Israelites temporary rest, whereas Jesus gives eternal rest (4:1-13). Jesus is greater than Aaron, Israel's first high priest, because of the covenant he effects, the ministry he has obtained, and the perfect sacrifice for sin he made (4:14–10:39). The writer closed by citing specific examples of men and women who received God's approval for living by faith (chap. 11), issuing a call for endurance (chap. 12), and giving some practical final exhortations (chap. 13).

Key Verses

"Long ago God spoke to the fathers by the prophets at different times and in different ways. In these last days, he has spoken to us by his Son. God has appointed him heir of all things and made the universe through him. The Son is the radiance of God's glory and the exact expression of his nature, sustaining all things by his powerful word. After making purification for sins, he sat down at the right hand of the Majesty on high. So he became superior to the angels, just as the name he inherited is more excellent than theirs" (Heb 1:1-4).

Food for Thought

No other book in the New Testament ties together Old Testament history, persons, events, institutions, and practices with the life of Jesus Christ as thoroughly as the book of Hebrews. The author of Hebrews wanted to exalt Jesus Christ. An important verbal indication of this desire was his consistent and repetitive use of the Greek word *kreittōn,* which means "more excellent," "superior," or "better" (1:4; 6:9; 7:7,19,22; 8:6; 9:23; 10:34; 11:16,35,40; 12:24). This word is the common thread that binds together the argument of the book.

Takeaway

In a culture that might at best acknowledge that Jesus is one of many ways to God, believers need to affirm clearly the superiority of Jesus to everyone and everything else and to be adamant that he is the full and ultimate revelation of God and the only Savior.

JAMES

Author

James the Just, the half brother of Jesus (1:1).

Date

Perhaps around AD 45.

Big Picture

True faith must be lived out in everyday life by good deeds; such good works demonstrate the presence of faith and justification before God.

Summary

After a brief salutation, James focused on the reality of trials. He invited his readers to see the trials they were undergoing as occasions for joy. Trials can build endurance, and endurance maturity. Trials also call for wisdom from God (1:1-18). God's Word needs to be heard and acted upon, for really hearing God's Word changes the way one speaks, how one treats vulnerable persons, and how one views persons considered inferior to oneself (chap. 2). James issued a warning about the potential evil of the tongue and what is required to bring it into check (3:1-12). Humbly acknowledging one's condition before God is an important step in diminishing arrogance, greed, and injustice toward others as well as in growing in the faith (3:13–5:12). James concluded his letter with some brief instruction about prayer and the importance of turning a fellow believer back to the truth (5:13-20).

Key Verses

"But someone will say, 'You have faith, and I have works.' Show me your faith without works, and I will show you faith by my works" (Jas 2:18).

"You see that a person is justified by works and not by faith alone" (Jas 2:24).

"For just as the body without the spirit is dead, so also faith without works is dead" (Jas 2:26).

Food for Thought

Many people believe that if in the end their good works outweigh their bad then God will accept them on judgment day. Many Christians are leery of talking about good works because they do not wish to leave the impression that good works are a means of salvation. Such believers rightly stress that salvation is by faith alone, apart from good works. But in a balanced Christianity good works are important. Good works are open to observation by others; faith is not. Therefore, good works make faith visible. Good works are never the root cause of salvation, but they are always the fruit, or result, of salvation.

Takeaway

If our profession of faith does not result in good works, we should evaluate the validity of our salvation experience.

1 PETER

Author

Simon Peter the apostle (1:1).

Date

Perhaps around AD 64.

Big Picture

Even though Christians may suffer for their faith, they are to live in holiness and humility while they wait for their great future hope of sharing Christ's glory; by doing so they will point others to the Lord.

Summary

Peter began his letter by reviewing believers' salvation. They were chosen by the Father, sanctified by the Spirit, and redeemed by the blood of Jesus. They now had a new birth, a living hope, and an indestructible inheritance. This salvation carried with it a call to a holy life and a place in God's spiritual house (1:1–2:12). Peter next focused on believers' submission, reminding his readers they were to follow Jesus's example (2:13–3:12). Third, Peter turned to believers' suffering. He warned them that while suffering may be intense, they should rely on God's grace, knowing that Christ also suffered unjustly and that there is a heavenly reward awaiting them. Suffering, however, did not excuse them from doing good (3:13–4:19). Finally, Peter addressed the shepherds of God's flock, instructing them about how they were to fulfill their roles and reminding them they had a Chief Shepherd to whom they were accountable (chap. 5).

Key Verses

"Rejoice as you share in the sufferings of Christ, so that you may also rejoice with great joy when his glory is revealed" (1 Pet 4:13).

"So then, let those who suffer according to God's will entrust themselves to a faithful Creator while doing what is good" (1 Pet 4:19).

Food for Thought

This book contains the most extensive New Testament development of a theology of suffering. The recipients of the letter are identified as sufferers in four of its five chapters. First Peter emphasizes that suffering is normal for believers because they are temporary residents in this alien world. As such, they lack rights and receive no justice in this foreign land. Though suffering occurs on earth for temporary residents, their inheritance and exaltation await them in their eternal homeland. Thus God's glory is served when his people suffer according to God's will (4:19).

Takeaway

When we suffer because of our Christian faith, we should draw strength from Christ's example and sufferings and continue to do good.

2 PETER

Author

Simon Peter the apostle (1:1).

Date

Perhaps around AD 67.

Big Picture

As Christians grow in understanding, they will be safeguarded from false teachers, especially those who deny the return of Christ and the end of the world as it now exists.

Summary

Peter began his letter by identifying eight qualities of Christian character that if increasing in believers' lives render them neither useless nor unfruitful (chap. 1). In chapter 2, Peter turned his attention to false teachers who were leading believers astray. These heretics' departure from sound teaching was motivated by greed and corrupt desires, and Peter warned of God's sure judgment. Peter finished his letter in chapter 3 by focusing on the day of the Lord and his return. The false teachers assumed there would be no accountability to God—no judgment. They pointed to how everything had continued on as it always had been. Peter told his readers that in God's time the universe as we know it will be destroyed and a "new heavens and a new earth, where righteousness dwells" will appear (3:13). Such a prospect carries with it the incentive to live a holy life.

Key Verses

"There were indeed false prophets among the people, just as there will be false teachers among you. They will bring in destructive heresies, even denying the Master who bought them, and will bring swift destruction on themselves" (2 Pet 2:1).

"Therefore, dear friends, since you know this in advance, be on your guard, so that you are not led away by the error of lawless people and fall from your own stable position" (2 Pet 3:17).

Food for Thought

In 3:17 Peter presented two options Christians face—then and now: either one goes forward in the faith, or one slips away from the faith. To put it another way, the safeguard against being led into error is to grow in the knowledge and understanding of the Lord and his ways. Since that is the case, believers should be intentional about their Christian growth. They should plan out ways by which such growth might occur—Bible reading and study, prayer, gathering with other believers, attending and listening to the proclamation and instruction of God's Word, ministering out of the spiritual gifts one has been given, and establishing an accountability relationship with a more spiritually mature believer who will guide, correct, and direct them in the faith.

Takeaway

Since there are real and serious dangers in false teaching, drawing on God's power, we are to do all we can to become mature followers of Jesus Christ.

1 JOHN

Author

Technically anonymous, but early Christian tradition identified John the apostle as the author.

Date

Perhaps around AD 80–90.

Big Picture

Christians have fellowship with Christ, who is God incarnate, and with other believers through having their sins forgiven, walking in the light, living in love, and holding to the truth; as a result, they can be assured they have eternal life.

Summary

John listed four reasons for writing his letter. First, he wrote to promote his readers' fellowship and joy (1:4). Such joy and fellowship are based on who God is and on what he has done for us in his Son, Jesus Christ (chap. 1). Second, John wrote to help readers avoid the pitfalls of sin yet find forgiveness when they stumbled (2:1). Third, John wrote to protect believers from false teachers (2:26). Their dangerous teachings denied that Jesus came with real humanity and a truly physical body and rejected Jesus as the Messiah (that he is the Christ). These heresies led to certain false behaviors, in particular a denial of the seriousness of sin (2:26–5:4). Finally, John wrote so his readers might know they have eternal life (5:13). This letter is a message of assurance.

Key Verses

"What we have seen and heard we also declare to you, so that you may also have fellowship with us; and indeed our fellowship is with the Father and with his Son Jesus Christ" (1 John 1:3).

"Dear friends, let us love one another, because love is from God, and everyone who loves has been born of God and knows God" (1 John 4:7).

"I have written these things to you who believe in the name of the Son of God so that you may know that you have eternal life" (1 John 5:13).

Food for Thought

John mentioned some form of the word *love* more than four dozen times in this short letter. He identified love as the ultimate test of the validity of one's Christian faith (3:14; 4:7-8). Such love in believers is called forth from God's nature (4:8,16) and from God's actions toward us (4:9,19). But believers' love is not only directed toward God; it includes fellow believers (3:14; 4:21). Believers show their love for God by loving one another. Where there is no love, there is no fellowship either with God or with others.

Takeaway

First John maps out three main components of saving knowledge of God: (1) faith in Jesus Christ, (2) obedient response to God's commands, and (3) love for God and others from the heart. A valid Christian faith must show evidence of all three.

2 JOHN

Author

Written by "the elder" (v. 1), whom early Christian tradition identified as John the apostle.

Date

Perhaps around AD 80–90.

Big Picture

Those who are faithful to Christ's teaching know the Father and the Son, and they one day will be fully rewarded.

Summary

John told his spiritual children to (1) walk in the truth, (2) obey God's commands, (3) love one another, and (4) guard the teachings of Christ so believers would not be deceived by false teaching. The deceivers denied the incarnation, that Jesus was God in the flesh (v. 7). Thus they were antichrist, against Christ. John also warned that if anyone helped or supported those who made such denials that such a person shared in the deceivers' evil work (v. 11). John confirmed the spiritual safety of the believing community with a beginning and ending reference to their election by God (vv. 1,13).

Key Verse

"Watch yourselves so you don't lose what we have worked for, but that you may receive a full reward" (2 John 8).

Food for Thought

A congregation can easily get off track. Second John reminds readers of the high priority of the most basic Christian outlook and activity—mutual love. Yet another priority is no less critical—true Christian teaching, especially about the person of Jesus Christ. This short letter strikes a strong blow for steadfastness. Those who heed its warning will take the right steps to "receive a full reward" (v. 8).

Takeaway

Only two commands appear in this second shortest book of the New Testament: a call to "watch yourselves" (v. 8) and the command "do not receive" those who plant false teaching (v. 10). As communities of faith, we must not allow "anyone who does not remain in Christ's teaching" (v. 9) to preach or teach, or if that person denies that Jesus Christ is God who became flesh (v. 7).

3 JOHN

Author

Written by "the elder" (v. 1), whom early Christian tradition identified as John the apostle.

Date

Perhaps around AD 80–90.

Big Picture

Christians are to recognize and to work for the truth of the gospel, and one way they do this is to show hospitality to Christian ministers who are hard at work for the Lord.

Summary

Four men and their reputations (growing out of their behavior) are the sum and substance of 3 John's subject matter. Gaius, the recipient of the letter, received a multifold commendation, words of exhortation and encouragement not to imitate the bad example of Diotrephes but instead to continue the good work he was doing in receiving and supporting the traveling teachers and missionaries (vv. 1-8). Diotrephes, the one causing trouble, is condemned for his high-handed and malicious autocratic actions (vv. 9-10). Demetrius, who was probably the bearer of the letter, is praised for his godliness (vv. 11-12). The fourth individual was the elder himself, into whose heart we get a glimpse (vv. 13-14).

Key Verses

"Therefore, we ought to support such people so that we can be coworkers with the truth" (3 John 8).

"Dear friend, do not imitate what is evil, but what is good. The one who does good is of God; the one who does evil has not seen God" (3 John 11).

Food for Thought

Personality conflicts in the church are nothing new. In Gaius we see a faithful leader devoted to the welfare of fellow believers, including supporting Christian workers financially. In Diotrephes we see a prima donna who loved to have public recognition, talked negatively against others, and sought to exercise total control in the congregation. In Demetrius we see one who was held in high esteem by all. We find these same personalities in the church today.

Takeaway

Truth is important. The words *truth* and *true* are used seven times in this shortest book of the New Testament, stressing the importance of Christians being committed to the truth, walking in the truth, and supporting those who minister the truth.

JUDE

Author

Jude, the half brother of Jesus (v. 1).

Date

Perhaps in the AD 60s.

Big Picture

Christians must defend the faith against false teaching and false teachers, and at the same time they must build up their own faith in Christ.

Summary

Jude originally had intended to write a letter on salvation to his dear friends. But he changed his plans when he learned of false teachers who had infiltrated the church (vv. 3-4). Because of their influence he instead urged his readers to contend for the faith (v. 3). Jude reminded his readers that they shared a common salvation and alerted them to the need for vigilance in contending for the faith. In verse 4, Jude introduced his readers to the opponents, pronounced judgment upon them, and outlined their vices. Verses 5-16 provide the evidence for what he said in verse 4. Jude closed this section with a reminder of the apostles' warnings that such false teachers would arise (vv. 17-19). In verses 20-23 Jude exhorted his readers to faithfulness and then closed with a doxology in verses 24-25.

Key Verse

"Dear friends, although I was eager to write you about the salvation we share, I found it necessary to write, appealing to you to contend for the faith that was delivered to the saints once for all" (Jude 3).

Food for Thought

Jude had intended to write a positive letter about the common salvation he and his readers shared. Instead, he had to pen a negative letter in which he condemned false teachers who were trying to persuade Christians that they were free to sin since they had been forgiven and were under God's grace. Thus this short letter reminds us there are times when even if we wish to have a positive ministry we must set that aside and focus on less pleasant matters, especially those ideas, teachings, and people who threaten the faith.

Takeaway

Though it is easier and more enjoyable to give positive feedback to our fellow Christians, there are times when we must address difficult and painful situations very directly.

REVELATION

Author
John the apostle (1:1,4,9).

Date
Around AD 95.

Big Picture
Jesus, the Lord of history, will return to earth, destroy all evil and all opposition to him, and bring the kingdom of God to its glorious culmination.

Summary
The book of Revelation previews its structure in 1:19: "Therefore write what you have seen, what is, and what will take place after this." John already had seen the vision of the exalted Son of Man clothed in power and majesty (chap. 1). Next, he was told to write letters to seven churches, telling each the state of its spiritual health (chaps. 2–3). In the body of the book (4:1–22:5) are a series of visions in which the glorified Christ revealed to John events related to the end times, covering all that would "take place after this." These chapters reveal God's judgments—represented under seven seals, seven trumpets, and seven bowls—on the earth and on all those opposed to him and the final triumph of the Lamb. The book ends with a vision of a new heaven and earth and John's plea for the Lord to "come" (chaps. 21–22).

Key Verses

"Look, he is coming with the clouds, and every eye will see him, even those who pierced him. And all the tribes of the earth will mourn over him. So it is to be. Amen" (Rev 1:7).

"The seventh angel blew his trumpet, and there were loud voices in heaven saying, 'The kingdom of the world has become the kingdom of our Lord and of his Christ, and he will reign forever and ever'" (Rev 11:15).

Food for Thought

The book of Revelation finishes the story begun in Genesis. Genesis focused on beginnings; Revelation focuses on consummation. In Genesis heaven and earth were created; in Revelation a new heaven and new earth appear (21:1). In Genesis the sun and moon appeared as the greater and lesser lights; in Revelation there is no longer any need of the sun or the moon, for the Lamb himself is the light (21:23; 22:5). In Genesis Eden was bounded by four rivers; in Revelation one river flows from God's throne through the center of the city. In Genesis God united Adam and Eve in marriage; in Revelation the marriage supper of the Lamb unites Christ and the church (19:6-9; 21:2). In Genesis Satan appeared as the adversary; in Revelation Satan is cast into the lake of fire (20:10). In Genesis sin entered the human race; in Revelation all sin is done away with (21:4,8). In Genesis death entered the human race; in Revelation there will be no more death (21:4). In Genesis the earth was placed under a curse; in Revelation the curse is lifted (22:3). In Genesis angelic beings blocked the entrance to the garden; in Revelation 12 angels are stationed at the never-closing gates of the new Jerusalem

(21:12). In Genesis humans were barred from the tree of life; in Revelation the tree of life bears fruit year-round for all the nations (22:2).

Takeaway

Since Jesus Christ will return, we are always to be ready for that great event.

ACKNOWLEDGMENTS

The Bible Guide draws on several B&H resources, especially the *Holman Illustrated Bible Handbook.* The core of the *Handbook* is taken from Kendell H. Easley's *QuickSource Guide to Understanding the Bible*, in which summaries of each of the Bible's sixty-six books are taken from *Holman Concise Bible Commentary*, David S. Dockery editor; *Holman Illustrated Bible Dictionary*, Chad Owen Brand, Charles W. Draper, Archie W. England, and Trent C. Butler, editors; *HCSB Apologetics Study Bible*, Ted Cabal, Chad Owen Brand, Ray Clendenen, Paul H. Copan, and J. P. Moreland, editors; *HCSB Study Bible*, Edwin A. Blum and Jeremy Royal Howard, general editors. Genesis: Eugene H. Merrill, Charles W. Draper, E. Ray Clendenen, Kenneth A. Mathews, A. Boyd Luter Jr., Robert D. Bergen; Exodus: Eugene H. Merrill, Trent C. Butler, Robert D. Bergen, Dorian G. Coover-Cox; Leviticus: Eugene H. Merrill, W. H. Bellinger Jr., Mark F. Rooker, Kenneth A. Mathews, Tiberius Rata; Numbers: Eugene H. Merrill, Douglas K. Wilson Jr., R. Dennis Cole; Deuteronomy: Eugene H. Merrill, Daniel I. Block; Joshua:

Kenneth A. Mathews, Stephen J. Andrews, Len Fentress, Richard S. Hess; Judges: Kenneth A. Mathews, Daniel I. Block, Barry C. Davis, Iain M. Duguid; Ruth: Kenneth A. Mathews, Daniel I. Block, Barry C. Davis, Iain M. Duguid; 1, 2 Samuel: Kenneth A. Mathews, Robert D. Bergen, Bryan E. Beyer; 1, 2 Kings: Kenneth A. Mathews, Pete Wilbanks, Phil Logan, Kirk E. Lowery, Andrew C. Bowling; 1, 2 Chronicles: Kenneth A. Mathews, John H. Traylor Jr., Kirk E. Lowery, Winfried Corduan; Ezra-Nehemiah: Kenneth A. Mathews, D. C. Martin, Barrett Duke, Carl R. Anderson; Esther: Kenneth A. Mathews, Kirk Kilpatrick, Barrett Duke, Carl R. Anderson; Job: Duane A. Garrett, Harry Hunt, Richard D. Patterson; Psalms: Duane A. Garrett, David M. Fleming, Russell Fuller, Allen P. Ross, Kevin R. Warstler, Sherri L. Klouda; Proverbs: Duane A. Garrett, Raymond C. Van Leeuwen, Edward M. Curtis, David K. Stabnow; Ecclesiastes: Duane A. Garrett, Stephen R. Miller; Song of Songs: Raymond C. Van Leeuwen, Sherri L. Klouda, Craig Glickman; Isaiah: Robert B. Chisholm, Harold Mosley, Steve Bond, Gary Smith, Tremper Longman III; Jeremiah: Robert B. Chisholm, Hans Mallau, E. Ray Clendenen, David K. Stabnow, Walter C. Kaiser; Lamentations: Robert B. Chisholm, David K. Stabnow, Walter C. Kaiser; Ezekiel: Robert B. Chisholm, Daniel I. Block, Lamar E. Cooper Sr., Mark F. Rooker; Daniel: Robert B. Chisholm, Stephen R. Miller, Michael Rydelnik; Hosea: E. Ray Clendenen, Billy K. Smith, Thomas J. Finley; Joel: E. Ray Clendenen, Alvin O. Collins, Thomas J. Finley, Shawn C. Madden; Amos: E. Ray Clendenen, Roy L. Honeycutt, Thomas J. Finley, Duane A. Garrett; Obadiah: E. Ray Clendenen, Leslie C.

Allen, Thomas J. Finley, Gregory W. Parsons; Jonah: E. Ray Clendenen, Thomas J. Finley, Joe Sprinkle; Micah: E. Ray Clendenen, Scott Langston, Thomas J. Finley, Kevin Peacock; Nahum: E. Ray Clendenen, Scott Langston, Thomas J. Finley, Gregory W. Parsons; Habakkuk: E. Ray Clendenen, John H. Tullock, Thomas J. Finley, Joe Sprinkle; Zephaniah: E. Ray Clendenen, Paul L. Redditt, Thomas J. Finley, Gregory W. Parsons; Haggai: E. Ray Clendenen, Thomas J. Finley, Gregory W. Parsons; Zechariah: E. Ray Clendenen, Thomas J. Finley, D. Brent Sandy; Malachi: E. Ray Clendenen, Thomas J. Finley; Matthew: Craig L. Blomberg, Oscar Brooks, Alan Hultberg, Charles L. Quarles; Mark: Christopher L. Church, Rodney Reeves, Alan Hultberg, Ross H. McLaren; Luke: Darrell L. Bock, T. R. McNeal, Alan Hultberg, A. Boyd Luter; John: James Emery White, C. Hal Freeman Jr., Craig L. Blomberg, Andreas Köstenberger; Acts: John Polhill, Charles W. Draper, Stanley E. Porter; Romans: David S. Dockery, Charles L. Quarles, William W. Klein, Edwin A. Blum; 1 Corinthians: David S. Dockery, R. E. Glaze, Paul W. Barnett, F. Alan Tomlinson; 2 Corinthians: David S. Dockery, R. E. Glaze, Paul W. Barnett, Kendell H. Easley; Galatians: David S. Dockery, C. Hal Freeman Jr., Walter Russell, A. Boyd Luter; Ephesians: David S. Dockery, Ray Summers, William W. Klein; Philippians: David S. Dockery, Michael Martin, Richard R. Melick Jr.; Colossians: David S. Dockery, Michael Martin, Clinton E. Arnold, Andreas Köstenberger; 1, 2 Thessalonians: David S. Dockery, Leon Morris, Michael W. Holmes, James F. Davis; 1, 2 Timothy: David S. Dockery, Mark E. Matheson, Charles L. Quarles, Ray Van Neste; Titus: David S. Dockery, Terry

L. Wilder, Charles L. Quarles, Ray Van Neste; Philemon: David S. Dockery, Kenneth Hubbard, Clinton E. Arnold, Murray J. Harris; Hebrews: Thomas D. Lea, Charles A. Ray, Terry L. Wilder, Malcolm B. Yarnell III; James: Thomas D. Lea, Paige Patterson, Terry L. Wilder, R. Gregg Watson; 1, 2 Peter: Thomas D. Lea, Thomas R. Schreiner, Terry L. Wilder; 1, 2, 3 John: Thomas D. Lea, Daniel L. Akin, Robert W. Yarbrough; Jude: Thomas D. Lea, Thomas R. Schreiner, Terry L. Wilder; Revelation: Robert B. Sloan, Daniel L. Akin, A. Boyd Luter Jr.

Additional resources are the introductory articles for the forthcoming CSB Study Bible by the following authors: Daniel I. Block, Kenneth H. Matthews, Duane A. Garrett, E. Ray Clendenen, Andreas J. Köstenberger, Charles L. Quarles, and George H. Guthrie; and Henrietta C. Mears, *What the Bible Is All About* (Mineapolis, MN: The Billy Graham Evangelistic Association, 1966).

SCRIPTURE INDEX